SOCIAL JUSTICE FALLACIES

SOCIAL JUSTICE

Fallacies

THOMAS SOWELL

BASIC BOOKS

New York

Basic Books
Hachette Book Group
1290 Avenue of the Americas, New York, NY 10104
www.basicbooks.com

Printed in the United States of America

First Edition: September 2023

Published by Basic Books, an imprint of Hachette Book Group, Inc. The Basic
Books name and logo is a trademark of the Hachette Book Group.

The Hachette Speakers Bureau provides a wide range of authors for speaking
events. To find out more, go to hachettespeakersbureau.com or email
HachetteSpeakers@hbgusa.com.

Basic Books copies may be purchased in bulk for business, educational, or promotional
use. For more information, please contact your local bookseller or the Hachette Book
Group Special Markets Department at special.markets@hbgusa.com.

The publisher is not responsible for websites (or their content) that are not owned by
the publisher.

Library of Congress Control Number: 2023941574

ISBNs: 9781541603929 (hardcover), 9781541603936 (ebook)

LSC-C

Printing 3, 2023

"You're entitled to your own opinion, but

you're not entitled to your own facts."

Daniel Patrick Moynihan

CONTENTS

Chapter 1

"EQUAL CHANCES" FALLACIES

Back in the eighteenth century, Jean-Jacques Rousseau expressed the essence of the social justice vision when he wrote of "the equality which nature established among men and the inequality which they have instituted among themselves."[1] In the kind of world envisioned by Rousseau, all classes, races and other subdivisions of the human species would have equal chances in all endeavors— *other things being equal.* But the more other things there are, influencing outcomes, the lower the chances of all those other things being equal.

In the real world, there is seldom anything resembling the equal outcomes that might be expected if all factors affecting outcomes were the same for everyone. Even in a society with equal opportunity— in the sense of judging each individual by the same standards— people from different backgrounds do not necessarily even *want* to do the same things, much less invest their time and energies into developing the same kinds of skills and talents.

In American sports, for example, blacks are very over-represented in professional basketball, whites in professional tennis, and Hispanics in Major League Baseball. In professional hockey, where there are more teams in the United States than in Canada, there are more Canadian players than American players— even though the population of the United States is more than eight times the population of Canada. There are also more hockey players from Sweden— nearly 4,000 miles away— in the NHL than there are hockey players from California, even though the population of California is nearly four times the population of Sweden.[2]

Different climates are among the many other things that are not equal. Colder climates, with waterways frozen for months at a time, offer more opportunities for more people to grow up developing the ice-skating skills essential for hockey. Such climates are far more common in

1

Canada and Sweden than in the United States in general or California in particular.

Climate differences are among numerous other differences that can facilitate the development of some capabilities in particular peoples and impede the development of other capabilities.

At the heart of the social justice vision is the assumption that, because economic and other disparities among human beings greatly exceed any differences in their innate capacities, these disparities are evidence or proof of the effects of such human vices as exploitation and discrimination.

These vices are in fact among the many influences that prevent different groups of people— whether classes, races or nations— from having equal, or even comparable, outcomes in economic terms or other terms. But human vices have no monopoly as causes of economic and other disparities.

It is especially difficult to make the case that inequalities of outcomes can be automatically assumed to have been caused by discrimination by dominant majorities against subordinate minorities, when in fact many subordinate minorities have economically outperformed dominant majorities in many countries around the world and in many periods of history.

A study of the Ottoman Empire, for example, found that none of the 40 private bankers listed in Istanbul in 1912 was a Turk, even though Turks ruled the empire. Nor was any of the 34 stockbrokers in Istanbul a Turk. Of the capital assets of 284 industrial firms in the Ottoman Empire, employing five or more workers, 50 percent of these firms were owned by Greeks and another 20 percent were owned by Armenians.[3]

The Ottoman Empire was by no means unique. Racial or ethnic minorities who have owned or operated more than half of whole industries in particular nations have included the Chinese in Malaysia,[4] Germans in Brazil,[5] Lebanese in West Africa,[6] Jews in Poland,[7] Italians in Argentina,[8] Indians in East Africa,[9] Scots in Britain,[10] Ibos in Nigeria,[11] and Marwaris in India.[12]

By contrast, we can read reams of social justice literature without encountering a single example of the proportional representation of different groups in endeavors open to competition— in any country in the world today, or at any time over thousands of years of recorded history.

Among the many factors that can prevent equal human *potentialities* from producing equally developed *capabilities* are factors over which humans have very little control— such as geography[13]— and other factors over which humans have no control at all, such as the past. There are innumerable things that can create unequal chances, some of which are worth examining in some detail.

To begin with a very mundane example of a demonstrable inequality of capabilities, most of the leading brands of beer in the United States were created by people of German ancestry.[14] China's Tsingtao beer was also created by people of German ancestry.[15] Germans have also been prominent among beer producers in Argentina,[16] Brazil[17] and Australia.[18] In Europe, Germany has long been the leading producer of beer.[19]

It so happens that Germans were producing beer back in the days of the Roman Empire.[20] When a particular people has been doing a particular thing for more than a thousand years, is it surprising if they tend to be more successful in that particular endeavor than others who have had no such history?

Here we are not discussing innate potential for achievements in general, but *developed capabilities* for doing very specific things. Whatever the combination of circumstances that may have led Germans to begin brewing beer in ancient times, the skills they developed over the many centuries since then are a fact of life today. The same is true of other groups that have developed particular skills in other particular endeavors in the past. One of many things that no individual, no institution and no society has any control over is the past. The past is irrevocable. And, as a noted historian said: "We do not live in the past, but the past in us."[21]

Germans are by no means unique in having particular things that they do better than many other peoples. Conversely, there are some things that other peoples do better than Germans. It is common, for example, to hear people speak of "French cuisine" or "Italian cuisine." But seldom— if ever— do people speak of "German cuisine" or "English cuisine." Yet these are all peoples in countries clustered together in Europe. Rome and Berlin are about the same distance from each other as New York and Chicago, while London and Paris are closer to each other than Los Angeles and San Francisco.

The point here is that, in what might seem like very similar circumstances, there can be very different histories, cultures and outcomes in particular endeavors. Particular groups having particular skills in particular kinds of endeavors have been a common fact of life over the centuries and in countries around the world.[22] Even if two groups happen to live in identical tangible surroundings today, how likely would they be to have had the same environmental influences throughout all the scores of millennia of human existence?

Scots have long been internationally renowned for the quality of the whisky they produce, as the French have been for their wines. But the Scots cannot match the French in producing wine, because the grapes that grow in France do not thrive in Scotland's colder climate. There is no reason whatever why the Scots should be expected to be equal to the French in producing wine— or either of them equal to the Germans in producing beer.

Neither race nor racism, nor any other form of discrimination, is necessary to account for such reciprocal inequalities. Nor have those who automatically invoke discriminatory biases, as explanations for unequal outcomes, been able to cite any country, anywhere in the world, that has had the proportional demographic representation which they have made a criterion.

RECIPROCAL   INEQUALITIES

While group equalities in the same endeavors are by no means common, what is common are *reciprocal inequalities* among groups in different endeavors. The equality among different groups of human beings— presupposed by those who regard disparities in outcomes as evidence or proof of discriminatory bias— might well be true as regards innate potentialities. But people are not hired or paid for their innate potentialities. They are hired, paid, admitted to colleges or accepted into other desired positions on the basis of their *developed capabilities* relevant to the particular endeavor. In these terms, reciprocal inequalities might suggest equal potentialities, without providing any basis for expecting equal outcomes.

Even groups lagging in many kinds of achievement tend nevertheless to have some particular endeavors where they do not merely hold their own but *excel*. Groups lacking in their educational backgrounds, for example, may lag in many other endeavors, for which such a background is essential— and yet such generally lagging groups have often excelled in some other endeavors, where personal talent and dedication are key factors. Sports and entertainment have long been among such endeavors with high achievements for such American groups rising out of poverty as the Irish, blacks and Southern whites.[23]

While group equality— in either incomes or capabilities— is hard to find, it is also hard to find any ethnic or other large social group that has no endeavor in which it is above average.

Reciprocal inequalities abound— even when equality does not. As we have seen, different ethnic groups dominate different American sports. One consequence of this is that the degree of inequality of group representation in American sports as a whole is not as severe as in each individual sport. A similar principle applies, for similar reasons, in other endeavors, because of reciprocal inequalities.

If one looks at wealthy, historic individuals in commerce and industry, for example, one could find Jews far more widely represented among historic leaders in retailing, finance and garment production and sales than in the steel industry, automobile production or coal mining. In the professions as well, groups that have similar representation in the professions as a whole can have very different representations in particular professions, such as engineering, medicine or the law. Asian American professionals are not necessarily concentrated in the same professions as Irish American professionals.

Because of reciprocal inequalities, the more narrowly defined the endeavor, the less likely are different groups to be comparably represented. Yet crusaders for social justice often decry uneven representation of groups in an individual company, as evidence or proof of employer discrimination in that particular company.

When different peoples evolve differently in very different settings and conditions, they can develop different talents that create reciprocal inequalities of achievements in a wide range of endeavors, without necessarily creating equality, or even comparability, in any of those endeavors. Such reciprocal inequalities lend no support to theories of either genetic determinism or discriminatory biases as automatic explanations of inequalities.

Many assumptions and phrases in the social justice literature are repeated endlessly, *without any empirical test*. When women are statistically "under-represented" in Silicon Valley, for example, some people automatically assume that to be due to sex discrimination by Silicon Valley employers. It so happens that the work done in Silicon Valley is based on an application of engineering skills, including computer software engineering— and American women receive *less than 30 percent* of the degrees in engineering, whether at the college level or the postgraduate level.[24]

When American men receive *less than 20 percent* of the undergraduate degrees in education, and only 22 percent and 32 percent of master's degrees and doctoral degrees, respectively, in the same subject,[25] is it surprising that men are under-represented among school teachers and women are under-represented in engineering occupations?

Comparing the statistical representation of women and men in either of these occupations is like comparing apples and oranges, when their educational specializations are so different. These educational specialization decisions were usually made individually, years before either the women or the men reached an employer to begin a professional career.

A more general question arises when the incomes of women as a whole are compared to the incomes of men as a whole. This leaves out many specific differences in the life patterns of women and men.[26] One of the most basic of these differences is that women are full-time, year-round workers significantly less often than men. U.S. Census Bureau data show that, in 2019, there were 15 million more male, full-time, year-round workers than female, full-time, year-round workers.[27] The work patterns of women include more part-time work, and some whole years when many women are out of the labor force entirely, often due to staying home to take care of young children.[28]

When these and other differences in work patterns are taken into account, male-female differences in income shrink drastically, and in some cases reverse.[29] As far back as 1971, single women in their thirties who had worked continuously since leaving school were earning slightly *more* than men of the same description.[30]

When there are statistical differences in the representation of various ethnic groups, different patterns within these groups themselves are likewise often overlooked. A typical example of equating differences in demographic representation with employer discrimination was a headline in a San Francisco newspaper:[31]

> Why are Black and Latino people
> still kept out of tech industry?

Are Asians "kept out" of professional basketball or Californians "kept out" of the National Hockey League? Is equal demographic representation so widespread or so automatic in other endeavors that its absence in a particular endeavor can only be due to someone keeping particular people out?

As in the case of sex differences in demographic representation in an engineering endeavor, ethnic differences in educational qualifications for an engineering career are blatant. Asian Americans have more college degrees in engineering than either blacks or Hispanics,[32] each of whom outnumbers Asian Americans in the U.S. population. At the Ph.D. level, Asian Americans' engineering degrees outnumber the engineering Ph.D.s of blacks and Hispanics put together.[33]

Such ethnic disparities in engineering degrees are by no means peculiar to the United States. In Malaysia during the 1960s, members of the Chinese minority received 408 engineering degrees, while members of the Malay majority received just 4.[34]

When comparing different ethnic groups in a given endeavor, we are again comparing apples and oranges in terms of specialized education or other specialized preparations. In these circumstances, equal opportunity— in the sense of applying the same standards to everyone— does not produce equal outcomes, even if no one is "kept out." There is no way that the Chinese in Malaysia could "keep out" Malay students in universities run by Malays, and subject to the authority of the Malaysian government, also run by Malays.

The "disparate impact" standard, used by courts of law for determining employer discrimination, implicitly assumes something that no one can seem to find anywhere— equal demographic representation of different groups. Any number of scholarly international studies have found gross disparities common in countries around the world.[35] One of these studies concluded: "In no society have all regions and all parts of the population developed equally."[36]

Nevertheless, some Justices of the U.S. Supreme Court have accepted "disparate impact" statistics as evidence or proof of employer discrimination, even though the Supreme Court itself has had statistical disparities more extreme than the disparities used to charge employers with discrimination. For eight consecutive years— from 2010 to 2017— all Supreme Court Justices were either Catholic or Jewish,[37] in a country where Protestants outnumber Catholics and Jews combined.[38] Yet one of the most obvious reasons for doubting any negative intention or conspiracy is that these Justices were appointed by Presidents of both political parties, and all those Presidents were Protestants.

None of this denies that employer biases are a factor that can be, and has been, responsible for some disparities in employment outcomes. But human biases have no monopoly among the many things that prevent "equal chances."

ORIGINS OF INEQUALITIES

The question whether different social groups have equal or unequal capabilities in various endeavors is very different from the question whether racial or sexual differences create inherently different mental potential determined by genes. The genetic determinism assumption that reigned supreme among American intellectuals of the Progressive era in the early twentieth century is an irrelevant issue in this context, though it will be dealt with in Chapter 2, and has been dealt with more extensively elsewhere.[39]

If we assume, for the sake of argument, that every social group— or even every individual— has equal mental potential at the moment of conception, that would still not be enough to guarantee even equal "native intelligence" at birth, much less equally developed capabilities after growing up in unequal circumstances and/or being culturally oriented toward different goals in different fields.

Inequalities Among Individuals

Unequal circumstances begin in the womb. Research has shown nutritional differences among pregnant women reflected later in IQ differences among their children, when these children were old enough to be tested.[40] Mothers' intakes of various substances can have positive or negative effects on a child's IQ and general well-being.[41]

Even where we might reasonably expect to find the greatest equality of developed capabilities— among children born to the same parents and raised in the same home— research going back as far as the nineteenth century, and including countries on both sides of the Atlantic, has shown that children who are the first-born in their family have, as a group, higher average IQs,[42] a higher rate of college completion,[43] and are over-represented among high achievers in a variety of endeavors.[44]

In the United States, for example, a study found that more than half the National Merit Scholarship finalists were a first-born child, even in five-child families, as well as in two-child, three-child and four-child families.[45] In other words, in five-child families, the first-born was the finalist more often than the other four siblings combined. Other measures of educational success or career success have likewise shown the first-born— and an only child— to be over-represented among the top performers in various endeavors, whether in the United States or among top performers in other countries surveyed.[46]

The first-born, or an only child, can have the undivided attention of both parents during a child's crucial earliest development. This is something which later siblings obviously cannot have. Conversely, children raised where there is only one parent present have been found in a number of studies to have a higher incidence of many social problems— again, both in the United States and on the other side of the Atlantic.[47] Studies of boys raised without a father present have found them very much over-represented among people with pathologies ranging from truancy to murder.[48]

As one study put it, these pathologies were more highly correlated with fatherlessness than with any other factor, "surpassing even race and poverty."[49] Fatherless boys had a higher than average rate of incarceration, whether they were black or white, though the incidence of fatherless boys has been higher among blacks.[50] Not all differences between races are due to race— either in the sense of genetics or in the sense of racial discrimination.

Clearly, there were no "equal chances" for these boys, whether they were treated fairly or unfairly by people they encountered in institutions ranging from schools to police departments. Girls were also affected negatively, as reflected in such things as higher rates of teenage pregnancy, when raised by one parent.[51] Very similar patterns of pathology were found in England, where the ethnic makeup of the underclass population is very different from that in the United States.[52] In England, the underclass is predominantly white, but it shows many social patterns very similar to the social patterns of low-income blacks in the United States,[53] even though the English underclass has no "legacy of slavery" to be used as an automatic explanation.

When American children are raised in different social classes, with different child-rearing practices, the chances of these children growing up with equal capabilities in adulthood can be seriously reduced. Research has shown that children raised by parents with professional occupations hear more than three times as many words per hour as children raised in families on welfare. Moreover, these are far more often positive and encouraging words when the parents are professionals, and more often negative and discouraging words when the family is on welfare.[54]

Can anyone seriously believe that children spending their formative years growing up in homes this different are likely to be the same as others in school, on a job or elsewhere?

In putting assumptions to the test of facts, a clear distinction must be maintained between equal *potentialities* at the beginning of life and equally *developed capabilities* later on. Some social justice advocates may implicitly assume that various groups have similar developed capabilities, so that different outcomes appear puzzling. But, when it comes to actual performance capabilities, a man is not even equal to himself— either physically or mentally— at different stages of his life, much less equal to all other people in their varying stages of life.

Inequalities Among Groups

The seemingly invincible fallacy at the heart of the social justice vision is that large categories of people— classes, races, nations— would tend to be either equal, or at least comparable, in their outcomes in various endeavors, if it were not for some discriminatory bias that has intervened to produce the large disparities we see around us.

Yet different groups, with different median ages— *varying by a decade or two*— are unlikely to be equal in endeavors requiring either the physical vitality of youth or the experience that comes with age. When Japanese Americans have a median age of 52 and Mexican Americans have a median age of 28,[55] their different representation in different occupations and at different income levels is hardly surprising. If these two groups were identical in every other respect, age differences alone would still be enough to make them differ in incomes, since middle-aged Americans have higher median incomes than Americans in their twenties.[56]

With nations— as with classes, races or ethnic groups— age differences alone are enough to make equal economic or other outcomes very unlikely. There are whole nations whose populations have a median age over 40 (Germany, Italy, Japan), and other nations whose median ages are under 20 (Nigeria, Afghanistan, Angola).[57] Why should anyone expect a nation where half the population are infants, young children and teenagers to have the same work experience and education— the same human capital— as a nation where half the population is 40 years old or older?

Different nations are also located in different geographic, climatic and other settings, with different advantages and disadvantages. Even if their populations had identical potential, they could hardly be expected to have equally developed capabilities, after centuries of being confronted with the task of surviving and evolving in very different settings around the world.

Whole continents differ greatly from one another. Although Africa is more than twice the size of Europe, the European coastline is thousands of kilometers longer than the African coastline.[58] This might seem to be almost impossible. But the European coastline has innumerable twists and turns, creating harbors where ships can dock safely, sheltered from the rough waters of the open seas. These harbors are an even bigger advantage than the longer coastline as such.

The European coastline is also increased by the many islands and peninsulas that make up more than one-third of that continent's total land area.[59] By contrast, the African coastline is smooth, with far fewer harbors and far fewer islands and peninsulas— which make up only 2 percent of Africa's land area.[60]

Is it surprising that Europeans have long had the benefit of far more maritime trade than Africans? Adam Smith noted this geographic difference back in the eighteenth century,[61] and he also rejected claims that Africans were racially inferior.[62] Other scholars have likewise described the numerous and severe geographic handicaps of sub-Saharan Africa especially.[63] Distinguished French historian Fernand Braudel concluded: "In understanding Black Africa, geography is more important than history."[64]

Harbors are just one of the various kinds of navigable waterways with major implications for the economic and social development of human beings. That is because of the enormous difference in costs between water transportation and land transportation. In the ancient world, for example, the cost of transporting a cargo across the length of the Mediterranean Sea—more than 2,000 miles— was less than the cost of transporting that same cargo just 75 miles inland.[65] This meant that people living on the coast had a vastly larger range of economic and social interactions with other coastal people and places than people living inland had with other people living inland or with their coastal compatriots.

A geographic treatise noted that, in ancient times, Europe's Mediterranean hinterland was "lingering in a backward civilization as compared with the Mediterranean coastland."[66] Nor was this peculiar to the Mediterranean region. It has been common in various parts of the world that "the coasts of a country are the first part of it to develop, not an indigenous or local civilization, but a cosmopolitan culture, which later spreads inland from the seaboard."[67] There have been special exceptions, but this has been a general pattern.[68]

This pattern reflected the great difference between the cost of water transportation and land transportation, which in turn affects economic prospects in many ways. Most of the large cities around the world are located on navigable waterways, because transporting the huge volume of food required to keep people fed in those cities would be enormously more expensive if all food had to be transported solely over land— especially before the modern invention of railroads and trucks during the past two centuries. Even today, places with access to navigable rivers have great economic advantages, especially if these are navigable rivers that connect to coastal areas.[69]

Climate is another aspect of nature that can influence the economic and social development of human beings. Fertile soils are found more often in the temperate zones than in the tropics.[70] This obviously affects the productivity of agriculture. But its effects do not end there. Urbanization depends on food supplied from outside urban communities, with agriculture usually being the primary source. Over the centuries, a wholly disproportionate share of advances in science, technology and other endeavors have originated in urban communities.[71]

An empirical study at Harvard's Center for International Development found that places in the temperate zone, with fertile soil and located within 100 kilometers of the sea, were 8 percent of the world's inhabited land area. But such places had 23 percent of the world's population and produced 53 percent of the world's Gross Domestic Product.[72] This is reflected in worldwide differences in income per person between such places and the rest of the world.[73]

This is just one of many differences among the world's geographic regions. When Europeans arrived in the Western Hemisphere, the indigenous peoples had no horses, oxen, camels or elephants, nor any other heavy-duty draft animals or beasts of burden to provide transportation for people and cargoes, such as animals provided in much of the Eastern Hemisphere. Llamas existed in the Inca empire in part of South America, where they were used as beasts of burden. But even in that fraction of South America where llamas existed, they were not large enough to be comparable to the animals used in the other half of the world.

The dearth of draft animals and beasts of burden in the Western Hemisphere had wider economic implications.   By making land transportation even more costly than usual, the lack of animals limited the distances where it was economically feasible to transport cargoes. This in turn also limited the size of vessels for water transportation. Canoes were common in the Western Hemisphere. But vessels of the size of European ships, or the even larger ships in China during Europe's Middle Ages, were not economically viable without animals to transport the vast cargoes, from miles around, required to fill such ships.

Nor were wheeled vehicles used in the Western Hemisphere before Europeans arrived. The wheel has sometimes been considered an epoch-making invention for economic development. But wheeled vehicles, without animals to pull them, had no such potential. The Mayans invented wheels, but they were used on children's toys.[74] Had the Mayans been in communication with the Incas and their llamas, conceivably wheeled vehicles, pulled by animals, might have become an economic asset in the Western Hemisphere. But geographic limitations on the size of a cultural universe in the Western Hemisphere at that time prevented the creation of such a development.

When the British confronted the Iroquois in North America, these were peoples drawing upon very different-sized cultural universes. Although the Iroquois were a confederation of tribes living in a large area, the animals present on the vast Eurasian landmass— and absent in the Western Hemisphere— gave the British access to the inventions, discoveries and knowledge from far wider regions of the world. The British were able to navigate across the ocean by using the compass, invented in China, steering with rudders invented in China, doing calculations with mathematical concepts from Egypt, using a numbering system invented in India, and writing on paper invented in China, using letters created by the Romans.

The Iroquois had no comparable access to the cultural achievements of the Incas or the Mayans.[75] Nor did they have as wide an exposure to the many diseases that spread across the vast Eurasian landmass— spanning more than 10,000 kilometers— creating devastating epidemics in centuries past, but leaving the surviving populations in Europe with biological resistance to many diseases, whose germs they took with them to the Western Hemisphere. There those diseases devastated many indigenous populations, who lacked biological resistance to those diseases. Death rates, sometimes exceeding 50 percent or more, among the indigenous peoples facilitated the European conquest of North and South America.

Neither with geographic factors nor other aspects of nature can we automatically assume either equal or random outcomes among human beings. There are too many factors at work to expect them all to be equal, or to have remained equal over the thousands of years in which human beings have developed economically and socially.

Nature— as exemplified by such things as differences in geography, climate, diseases and animals— has *not* been egalitarian, despite Rousseau's claim that nature produced equality. As distinguished economic historian David S. Landes put it, "nature like life is unfair"[76] and "The world has never been a level playing field."[77]

Numerous geographic influences, varying from place to place, do not imply geographic determinism. These and other factors interact with human knowledge and human errors, as these have developed in different eras. Famines have occurred in places where there was very fertile land that produced food surpluses for export, both before the famine and after the famine.[78] The supply of natural resources is not fixed, because what is a natural resource depends on what human beings know how to use, and that changes with changes in human knowledge from one era to the next.

Western Europe and Northern Europe have long had more of the natural resources used in an industrial revolution— iron ore and coal, for example— than did Eastern Europe or Southern Europe. But none of that mattered during the many thousands of years before human beings' knowledge developed to the point where they were capable of creating an industrial revolution. Which part of Europe was more advantaged or disadvantaged varied with particular eras, and the human knowledge available in those eras.

Nature has been no more fair between the sexes than in its treatment of other social groups, societies or nations. Human double standards of sexual behavior for women and men have been a pale reflection of nature's more fundamental double standards. No matter how reckless, selfish, stupid or irresponsible a man may be, he will never become pregnant. The plain and simple fact that women have babies has meant that they may not have equal chances in many other aspects of life, even when some human societies offer equal opportunity for people with the same developed capabilities.[79]

The seemingly invincible fallacy that only human bias can explain different economic and social outcomes among peoples is belied repeatedly by hard facts in societies around the world. Whatever the condition of human beings at the beginning of the species, scores of millennia had already come and gone before anyone coined the phrase "social justice."

During those almost unimaginably vast expanses of time, different peoples evolved differently in very different settings around the world— developing different talents that created *reciprocal inequalities* of achievements in different endeavors, without necessarily creating equality, or even comparability, in any of those endeavors.

Environment and Human Capital

Environment cannot be defined as simply the current tangible surroundings. Nor can human capital be defined as simply education or skills. Qualities such as honesty are not only moral virtues for individuals, but human capital for communities, their cultures and their economies.

Where a geographic setting offers only limited and isolated patches of marginally fertile land that can sustain only small communities living close to the margins of subsistence, there is little to gain from deception and everything to lose if the people in that environment do not stick together and be honest with one another, for the sake of the mutual trust and cooperation required for their survival, in circumstances where survival is by no means secure.

People living for centuries in small, poor and isolated communities, with neither police forces nor fire departments, know that any emergency can become a catastrophe, unless they all stick together and come to each other's rescue. Such circumstances— obvious to those who live in these circumstances— can promote honesty and cooperation more than any preaching or laws. Other people in very different and more favorable circumstances may or may not develop a comparable sense of honesty and cooperation.

In short, honesty is one of many factors that cannot be assumed to be equally present in all places or among all peoples. Nor does empirical evidence suggest an equality in this factor, any more than in many other factors. Among the simple tests used to assess the honesty in various peoples and places have been projects that deliberately left wallets containing both money and personal identification in public places in various cities around the world.

When one such project in 2013 left a dozen wallets in public places, in various cities, the number of wallets returned with the money still in them varied from eleven out of twelve in Helsinki (Finland) to one out of twelve in Lisbon (Portugal). Moreover, the one wallet that was returned in Lisbon was returned by a couple visiting from the Netherlands; no Portuguese returned any.[80] An earlier test found 100 percent of the wallets returned in Norway, 67 percent in the United States, 30 percent returned in China and 21 percent returned in Mexico.[81]

A different test of honesty was a five-year study of which United Nations diplomats paid their parking tickets in New York City, where diplomatic immunity shielded them from prosecution. Egypt, with 24 U.N. diplomats, had thousands of unpaid parking tickets during that five-year period. Meanwhile, Canada— with the same number of U.N. diplomats as Egypt— had no unpaid parking tickets at all during that same five-year period. Nor did Britain, with 31 U.N. diplomats or Japan with 47 U.N. diplomats.[82]

John Stuart Mill pointed out in the nineteenth century that the level of honesty or dishonesty in a society was a major factor in the development of its economy. Using the high level of corruption in Russia as an example, Mill concluded that it must be "an immense drag on the capabilities of economical improvement."[83] Since then— whether under the czars, the communists or in post-communist Russia— corruption has been pervasive.[84] At one time, some individuals were described by fellow Russians as being "as honest as a German"[85]— a tacit admission that such qualities were not nearly as common among Russians.

Conversely, the industrial revolution in England was aided by investments from foreign countries, whose investors were able to rely on the reputation of British law for honesty and impartiality.

There is no more reason to expect all individuals, groups or nations to be equally honest than there is to expect them to have the same skills, the same wealth or the same IQs.

Even in countries with widespread corruption, where what has been called "the radius of trust" seldom extends beyond the nuclear family, there can be particular groups who have sufficient trust among themselves that they can conduct business on the basis of verbal agreements, without recourse to unreliable legal systems. Marwaris in India and various sub-groups among the overseas Chinese in Southeast Asia have even been able to engage in international trade with members of their own groups in other countries, on the basis of verbal understandings.[86]

This can be an enormous competitive economic advantage in countries with unreliable legal and political institutions, when indigenous rivals have to be far more cautious about economic transactions. But, even in a country with more reliable institutions, there are advantages in being able, as Hasidic Jews in New York are, to give each other consignments of jewels to sell, and share the profits on the basis of verbal agreements.[87]

Whatever the level of honesty in a given society, there is no reason to expect existing disparities in these respects to remain the same forever, when so many other things have changed over the centuries. But, at any given time, honesty is one of many factors that vary, making equal chances for all very unlikely.

Episodic Factors

In addition to on-going differences among peoples, there have also been unpredictable episodic events— such as wars, famines, and epidemics— that can disrupt the development path of particular peoples. The outcomes of military conflicts can be a matter of chances that are incalculable— and yet able to determine the fate of whole societies or nations for subsequent generations or centuries.

Had Napoleon won the battle of Waterloo, instead of his enemy the Duke of Wellington, the history of peoples and nations across the continent of Europe could have been very different. Wellington himself said afterwards that the outcome of that battle was "the nearest run thing you ever saw in your life."[88] It could have gone either way. Had the earlier battle against invading Islamic forces at Tours in 732 or at the siege of Vienna in 1529 gone the other way, Europe would be culturally a very different place today.

As things turned out, Europe has been far from being a culturally, economically or otherwise homogeneous civilization, with its peoples having the same quantity and kind of human capital across the continent. Instead, the languages of Western Europe acquired written versions centuries before the languages of Eastern Europe.[89] This had major implications for the education of the peoples in these two regions, who had little chance to be equal in endeavors requiring the kinds of knowledge and skills taught from books in schools and colleges.

This was not simply an inequality confined to the past, for the evolution to the present began from very different pasts in different places and times. Eastern Europe has been poorer and less industrially developed than Western Europe for centuries,[90] and the homicide rate in Eastern Europe has been some multiple of the homicide rate in Western Europe for centuries.[91]

Nor was this east-west divide the only source of national inequalities within Europe. At the beginning of the twentieth century, "when only 3 percent of the population of Great Britain was illiterate, the figure for Italy was 48 percent, for Spain 56 percent, for Portugal 78 percent."[92] There were similar disparities in 1900 within the Habsburg Empire, where the rate of illiteracy ranged from 3 percent in Bohemia to 73 percent in Dalmatia.[93] Massive scholarly studies have found great differences in both technological development and in the number of leading figures in the arts and sciences in different parts of Europe.[94]

It was much the same story in Africa, where in 1957 only 11 percent of the children attending secondary school in Nigeria were from the northern part of the country, where a majority of the population lived.[95] Someone born in northern Nigeria had nowhere near the same chances as someone born in southern Nigeria— a fact reflected in the different economic success of tribes from these different regions of the country.[96]

Both in Europe and in Nigeria, different circumstances led different groups to different levels of literacy and different school attendance. In Europe— in centuries past, when people were far poorer— some groups working in agriculture had little need for literacy, but often had great need for the work of children, in order to keep families adequately fed. In such circumstances, children's education was often sacrificed, depriving them of even second-hand knowledge of a wider world.

In other parts of the world as well, innumerable factors influenced the development of innumerable peoples. It would be an incredible coincidence if all these factors affected all these peoples the same way during the many thousands of years in the past. What is also very unlikely, over vast expanses of time, is that the very same peoples would have been the highest achievers throughout many thousands of years. Just within a fraction of those millennia for which there has been recorded history, the peoples who have been in the forefront of human achievements have changed dramatically.

For centuries, China was far more technologically advanced than any European nation— having cast iron a thousand years before the Europeans.[97] The Chinese also had mechanical printing on paper, during centuries when Europeans were still writing by hand on costlier materials.[98] Educating most Europeans with costly individual manuscripts, rather than mass-produced books, was not an economically viable prospect. Only after Europeans developed mechanical printing themselves was it feasible for them to educate more than a small fraction of their populations. And only after all the languages of different European peoples developed written versions was an equal education, and the development of equal human capital, even theoretically possible.

Differences in human capital— including honesty and languages, as well as occupational skills and industrial and commercial talents— have been common between nations and within nations. There was no way that people on the short end of these circumstantial disparities had "equal chances" of developing their capabilities, even in a society with equal opportunity, in the sense of open competition for all, and equal standards applied to all.

We might agree that "equal chances for all" would be desirable. But that in no way guarantees that we have either the knowledge or the power required to make that goal attainable, without ruinous sacrifices of other desirable goals, ranging from freedom to survival.

Do we want the mixture of students who are going to be trained to do advanced medical research to be representative of the demographic make-up of the population as a whole— or do we want whatever students, from whatever background, who have track records demonstrating a mastery of medical science that gives them the highest probability of finding cures for cancer, Alzheimer's and other devastating diseases? *Endeavors have purposes.* Is indulging ideological visions more important than ending cancer and Alzheimer's?

Do you want airlines to have pilots chosen for demographic representation of various groups, or would you prefer to fly on planes whose pilots were chosen for their mastery of all the complex things that increase your chances of arriving safely at your destination? Once we recognize the many factors that can create different developed capabilities, "equal chances for all" becomes very different in its consequences from "equal opportunity." And consequences matter— or should matter— more so than some attractive or fashionable theory.

More fundamentally, do we want a society in which some babies are born into the world as heirs of pre-packaged grievances against other babies born the same day— blighting both their lives— or do we want to at least leave them the option to work things out better in their lives than we have in ours?

Chapter 2

RACIAL FALLACIES

R acial and ethnic issues have often produced vehement assertions in various times and places around the world. These assertions have ranged from the genetic determinism of early twentieth-century America— which proclaimed that "race is everything"[1] as an explanation of group differences in economic and social outcomes— to the opposite view at the end of that century that *racism* was the primary explanation of such group differences.

That different people have different beliefs is hardly unusual in the history of human beings. What is unusual— and dangerous— is (1) the extent to which such beliefs prevail without being subjected to tests of either facts or logic, and (2) the extent to which people who present empirical evidence counter to prevailing beliefs are met with *ad hominem* denunciations and with efforts to suppress their evidence, by means ranging from censorship to violence, especially on academic campuses.

These are not simply dangers to particular individuals or particular viewpoints. These are dangers to the basic functioning of a free society of fallible human beings, whose differing beliefs must be put to some test. Otherwise, a free society can either destroy freedom or destroy itself in internal conflict. Both have happened all too often, in all too many places, over the centuries.

ASSERTIONS VERSUS EVIDENCE

The fundamental issue is *not* whether employer discrimination— or societal discrimination in general— can be a cause of different economic and social outcomes among racial or ethnic groups. It can be, it has been, and there is no reason whatever to preclude it from the possibilities in our own times. But there is also no reason to preclude any of the many other factors that have also produced outcome disparities among all sorts of groups, around the world and throughout recorded history.

Since the most often discussed disparities in the United States have been disparities between black and white Americans, this is as good a place to begin as any. The question is whether differences between black and white Americans are unusual, or are of an unusually larger magnitude than differences among other groups in the United States or elsewhere. The question is also whether there are any other discernible reasons for those differences besides race— that is, genetics— or racism.

Median black American family income has been lower than median white American family income for generations. As regards the magnitude of the difference, official government data going back as far as 1947 show that the disparity has not been as large as 2:1 in any of those years.[2] How does that particular disparity compare to disparities among other groups in the United States, or among groups in other countries?

Within the United States, the median per capita income of such Asian ethnic groups as those of Chinese, Japanese, Indian and Korean ancestry is *more* than twice as high as the median per capita income of Mexican Americans.[3] These Asian groups also have higher median per capita incomes than the median per capita income of white Americans.[4] Asian Indians have nearly *three times* the median per capita incomes of Mexican Americans, and a median per capita income more than $15,000 a year higher than the median per capita income of white Americans.[5] Among full-time, year-round male workers, Asian Indian males earned over $39,000 a year *more* than white male full-time, year-round workers.[6]

Is this the "white supremacy" we are so often warned about in some quarters? Even among low-income, non-white groups, there is considerable overlap with the incomes of white Americans. For example, 2020 census data show more than 9 million black Americans with higher incomes than the median incomes of white Americans.[7] There are also thousands of black millionaire families,[8] and even several black billionaires, including Tiger Woods and Oprah Winfrey.[9]

However much this situation differs from the image of blacks in political rhetoric, and in much of the media and academia— an image that often seems more like what existed a century ago— the current situation is no reason for complacency. On the contrary, it is a reason for a younger generation of blacks to educate themselves for opportunities that are clearly available, and to advance themselves even more than previous generations of black people have.

Nevertheless, economic differences between different groups are a special concern when discussing different rates of poverty. For example, the poverty rate among black American families as a whole has long been higher than the poverty rate among white American families as a whole.[10] But, over a span of more than a quarter of a century since 1994, in no year has the annual poverty rate of black *married-couple* families been as high as *10 percent*. And in no year in more than half a century since 1959 has the national poverty rate of Americans as a whole been as *low* as 10 percent.[11]

If black family poverty is caused by "systemic racism," do racists make an exception for blacks who are married? Do racists either know or care whether blacks are married?

By contrast, single-parent families have much higher poverty rates than married-couple families— whether they are black or white. White, female-headed, single-parent families have had a poverty rate *more than double* the poverty rate of black married-couple families in every year from 1994 to 2020, the latest year for which data are currently available.[12] If "white supremacists" were so powerful, how could this happen?

Male-headed, single-parent families are rarer than female-headed, single-parent families, among both blacks and whites. White, male-headed, single-parent families have had a lower rate of poverty than white, female-headed, single-parent families. Nevertheless, white, male-headed, single-parent families have also had a *higher* poverty rate than black married-couple families, in every year from 2003 to 2020.[13]

Statistical differences between races are not automatically due to race— either in the sense of being caused by genetics or being a result of racial discrimination. Differences in the proportion of single-parent families among various racial groups are other differences that affect differences in income. So are differences in median age, and in education— among other factors.

Just as income disparities are by no means unique among American racial or ethnic groups, neither are disparities *within* such groups necessarily any less than disparities *between* these groups.

In New York City, for example, in school year 2017–2018 there were dozens of places in low-income minority neighborhoods where public charter schools and traditional public schools, serving the same local community, were housed in the same buildings. When black and Hispanic students in both kinds of schools took the same statewide test in mathematics, the charter school students achieved the official "proficient" level in mathematics *more than 6 times as often* as children of the same ethnicities in traditional public schools housed in the very same buildings.[14] These are huge disparities *within* the same groups, so that neither race nor racism can account for these huge differences.[15] Nor can culturally biased tests.

Similarly, a 1930s study of the black community in Chicago found that the delinquency rate within that community ranged from more than 40 percent in some black neighborhoods to less than 2 percent in some other black neighborhoods.[16] Again, these were disparities *within* the same racial group in the same city at the same time.

Within the white population as well, there have long been internal disparities as great as the disparities between blacks and whites. In 1851, for example, when the white population of the South was about half as large as the white population in other regions, only 8 percent of the patents issued in the United States went to residents of the Southern states.[17] Southern whites also long lagged behind other whites in various work skills. For example, although the South in 1860 had 40 percent of the nation's dairy cows, they produced just 20 percent of the nation's butter and only 1 percent of the nation's cheese.[18] Southerners' lags in the dairy industry continued on into the twentieth century.[19]

In addition to such quantifiable differences as a higher rate of illiteracy among Southern whites in the antebellum South than among their Northern white contemporaries,[20] many observers commented on a visibly lower work effort among Southern whites. These observers included Alexis de Tocqueville, in his classic *Democracy in America*[21] and

Frederick Law Olmsted in his widely read account of his travels in the antebellum South, *The Cotton Kingdom*.[22] Among white Southerners themselves, similar observations were made by General Robert E. Lee,[23] antebellum Southern writer Hinton Helper[24] and twentieth-century Southern historians U.B. Phillips[25] and Rupert B. Vance.[26]

Even today, in the twenty-first century, there are counties in the Appalachian regions of Kentucky— Clay County and Owsley County— that are more than 90 percent white, where the median household income is not only less than half the median household income of white Americans in the country as a whole, but also thousands of dollars less than the median household income of *black* Americans in the country as a whole.[27] A Census Bureau study found Owsley County to be the lowest-income county in any American state in 2014, and its population was 99 percent white.[28]

These were not just isolated flukes in a particular year. These very same counties had the very same income pattern in five different surveys, made over more than half a century, during the years from 1969 to 2020.[29]

In 2014, an article in the *New York Times Magazine* rated American counties in economic terms— and six of the bottom ten counties were in eastern Kentucky.[30] Although that article did not mention the race of the people in those counties, Census data show that each of these six counties had populations that were more than 90 percent white.[31]

Here too, this was not just a fluke in a particular year. Data for these same six counties, surveyed over the same years from 1969 to 2020, show a very similar pattern of median household incomes consistently far below the median household income of whites nationwide, as well as median household incomes consistently below the median household incomes of blacks nationwide.[32]

In a sense, such patterns go back even further. More than a hundred years ago, a scholarly treatise on geography pointed out how people of the same race, living in different geographic settings, can have radically different economic and social outcomes— using Kentucky communities among the examples. This treatise referred to the "hill country of the Cumberland Plateau," with its "one-room cabins" and "a backward population sprung from the same pure English stock as the Bluegrass people."[33] Nor was this pattern peculiar to the United States.

According to the author, distinguished geographer Ellen Churchill Semple, such "influences of environment" appear "in every part of the world, in every race and every age."[34] Her own voluminous research, and that of other scholars since then, show that people living in mountains and foothills— "hillbillies" in American terminology— have usually lagged both economically and in terms of social development.[35] High levels of high-school dropouts and low levels of college graduates among American hillbillies are obvious examples of neglected social development.

What we learn from persistent and severe poverty in hillbilly communities can be helpful in sorting out factors involved in the poverty and lagging progress of other peoples, including racial minorities. If, by some miracle, we could get to zero racism, it is by no means certain how much effect that would have. People in low-income American hillbilly counties already face zero racism, because these people are virtually all white. Yet they have lower incomes than blacks.

Conversely, in a world where nobody believes that all racism has been eliminated, black married couples have consistently had a lower poverty rate than the national average, and less than half the poverty rate among white, female-headed, single-parent families. In other words, *some behavior patterns seem to pay off,* more so than an absence of racism.

Some emphasis on racism can even be counterproductive. President Barack Obama related an experience he had when talking with a black young man who wanted to become a pilot. This young man at first thought of joining the U.S. Air Force, in order to get trained to be a pilot. But then he said he realized that the Air Force "would never let a black man fly a plane."[36] This was said *decades after there was a whole squadron of black American fighter pilots during World War II*— and, in later years, two black pilots went on to become *generals* in the U.S. Air Force.[37] Whoever indoctrinated this young man did him more harm than a racist could have, by keeping him from even trying to become a pilot.

There are many reasons why different people are in poverty, and these reasons are not limited to just the ones that happen to be currently in vogue, such as discrimination by race or sex. None of this automatically tells us how much effect discrimination, or any other factor, has on a given group's economic or other advancement, which can vary at different times or under different conditions. But the facts of history can at least save us from jumping to automatic conclusions, on the basis of rhetoric and repetition of such catchwords as "legacy of slavery," "white supremacy," and "blaming the victim."

Alexis de Tocqueville set an unfortunate precedent, in the early nineteenth century, when he attributed differences between Southern whites and Northern whites to the existence of slavery in the South[38]— a view echoed by both Frederick Law Olmsted[39] and Hinton Helper.[40] In reality, however, the very same range of differences existed between the ancestors of white Southerners and the ancestors of white Northerners when they lived in different parts of Britain, before either of them had ever seen a slave.[41] The very same unsubstantiated assumption would be used again in the twentieth century, and on into our own times, to try to explain behavioral differences between blacks and whites by "a legacy of slavery."

The higher incidence of children being born to unmarried women among black Americans is among many other things attributed to a "legacy of slavery." But, *for more than a hundred years* after the end of slavery, most black children were born to women who were married, and the children were raised in two-parent homes. Daniel Patrick Moynihan became alarmed, back in the 1960s, because 23.6 percent of black children were born to single mothers in 1963— and that was *up* from 16.8 percent in 1940.[42]

Although these rates for black Americans were much higher than for white Americans, the rate of births to unmarried women among whites also rose suddenly and sharply in the 1960s, after having been— for decades— only a small fraction of what it became after 1960.[43] For neither blacks nor whites does this pattern suggest a "legacy of slavery," when this upturn in births to unmarried women began for both races with the huge expansion of the welfare state in the 1960s. This new pattern has now persisted for more than half a century. In 2008, births to unmarried women among white Americans reached almost 30 percent.[44]

This exceeded the 1963 levels among black Americans that had alarmed Daniel Patrick Moynihan.[45]

The proportion of births to unmarried black mothers at the end of the twentieth century (68.7 percent)[46] still greatly exceeded the proportion among unmarried white mothers as a whole. But, among white mothers *with less than 12 years of education,* the rate of non-marital births in the early years of the twenty-first century was not far behind at just over 60 percent.[47]

As with other disparities, differences between races are not necessarily racial differences, either in the sense of being caused by genes or being caused by racial discrimination. Some behavioral patterns produce similar outcomes in groups that differ by race, so that these disparities in outcomes can reflect disparities in behavior— for whatever reasons— without implying either genetic determinism or societal discrimination. Internationally, in the twenty-first century, there are a number of European nations where at least 40 percent of the births are to unmarried women[48]— and these nations have no "legacy of slavery." But they have expanded welfare states.

Justice Oliver Wendell Holmes said, more than a century ago, that catchwords can "delay further analysis for fifty years."[49] Too many catchwords have already delayed analysis longer than that— and are still doing so.

GENETIC DETERMINISM

In the early decades of the twentieth century, when Progressivism was a major new force among American intellectuals and in politics, one of Progressivism's central tenets was genetic determinism— the belief that less successful races were genetically inferior.

Later, in the closing decades of the twentieth century, Progressives with similar views on such other issues as the role of government, environmental protection and legal philosophy, now took an opposite view on racial issues. Less successful races were now seen as being automatically victims of racism, as they had once been considered automatically inferior. The conclusions were different, but the way evidence was used and the way contrary views and contrary evidence were disregarded, was very similar.

Both sets of Progressives expressed utter certainty in their conclusions— on this and other subjects— and dismissed critics as uninformed at best, and confused or dishonest at worst.[50]

While Progressivism was an American movement, similar views and attitudes existed under other names on the other side of the Atlantic. There too, the prevailing views on race were opposite at the beginning of the twentieth century from what they became at the end of that century, and on into our own times.

Early Progressivism

Genetic determinism did not begin with the Progressives. In earlier times, many people considered themselves born inherently superior to other people, without requiring either the reality or the pretense of scientific evidence.

Some considered themselves superior as a class or a race, or because of royal blood, or whatever. In Britain, Sir Francis Galton (1822–1911) wrote a book titled *Hereditary Genius,* based on the fact that many outstanding achievements were concentrated in particular families. This conclusion might have had more weight as evidence if other families had comparable opportunities, but such a requirement could hardly have been met then, and it is not certain how often it can be met now.

A major piece of empirical evidence became available when soldiers in the U.S. Army were given mental tests during the First World War. Mental test scores from a sample of more than 100,000 of these tests showed that black soldiers as a whole scored lower than white soldiers as a whole on those tests. That was treated as irrefutable evidence that genetic determinism was a proven fact.[51] But an internal breakdown of the mental test score data showed that black soldiers from Ohio, Illinois, New York and Pennsylvania scored higher on the Army mental tests than white soldiers from Georgia, Arkansas, Kentucky and Mississippi.[52]

If the reason for the over-all test score differences between the races were genetic, people's genes do not change when they cross a state line. But some states do have better schools than others.

Even a moderately well-informed person in that era could hardly avoid knowing that other things were not equal between the races in the South, as Southern politicians of that era loudly proclaimed their determination to keep things unequal. This went beyond an unwillingness to spend equally on black and white schools. As far back as the end of the Civil War, when thousands of white volunteers from the North went into the South to teach the children of newly freed slaves, these teachers— mostly young women— were not only ostracized by Southern whites, but were even harassed and threatened.[53]

This was an era when many Southern whites did not want blacks to be educated, and the education policies of Southern state governments reflected that.[54] When wealthy white philanthropists such as John D. Rockefeller, Andrew Carnegie and Julius Rosenwald sent money to help create schools for black children in the South,[55] the state of Georgia passed a law, taxing donations to schools by people of a different race from the race of the students in those schools.[56]

The most fundamental problem with the conclusions reached by the genetic determinists of that era— and the opposite conclusions reached by Progressives of a later era— was in the way they used empirical evidence. Progressives in each era began with a preconception, and ended their examination of evidence when they found data which seemed to fit their preconception. Such a procedure may be enough to supply talking points. But, if the goal is to find the truth, the search must continue, in order to see if there are other data that conflict with the initial belief.

People with opposing views are often eager to supply opposing evidence, so the difficulty is not in finding such evidence. The difficulty is in whether such evidence will be examined. For example, were there other groups of whites— besides soldiers from certain states during the First World War— who scored as low on mental tests as blacks, or lower than blacks, in the twentieth century? It turns out that there were. These would include whites living in some American mountain and foothill communities.[57]

There have also been white people living in the Hebrides islands off Scotland,[58] and white people living in canal boat communities in Britain, with IQ test scores similar to those of black Americans.[59] What these particular whites have all had in common was *isolation*, whether geographic isolation or social isolation. Such social isolation from the larger society has also long been common among black Americans.

Although blacks in the U.S. Army during the First World War scored marginally lower than various members of recently-arrived European immigrant groups, other blacks— living in Northern communities— often scored either equally or marginally *higher* on mental tests than these same immigrant groups. These immigrants included Italian American children in a 1923 survey of IQs.[60] Similar results were found in a 1926 survey of IQ results for Slovaks, Greeks, Spaniards and Portuguese in the United States.[61] During this era, most European immigrants settled outside the South, and blacks outside the South had higher average IQs than blacks living in the South.[62]

Whites living in isolated mountain and foothill communities are an especially striking group, as regards poverty and isolation from both the outside world and from similar communities in the same mountains and foothills. We have seen how strikingly lower the incomes of such people have been in Appalachian counties in the twenty-first century.[63] Back in 1929, the IQs of children in Blue Ridge Mountain areas were studied, and can be compared to the IQs of blacks, which averaged 85 nationally. The average IQs of these white children in Blue Ridge Mountain communities ranged from a high of 83.9 to a low of 61.2, varying with which particular IQ test was used.[64]

White children in East Tennessee mountain schools in 1930 had an average IQ of 82.4. As with black children with similar IQs, these white mountain children had higher IQs when young— 94.68 at age six, declining to 73.50 at age sixteen.[65] A decade later, in 1940, after many improvements in both the local environment and in the schools, children in the same communities— and apparently from many of the same families[66]— had an average IQ of 92.22. Now their average IQ at age six was 102.56, and this declined to 80.00 at age sixteen.[67]

Clearly, these lower than average IQs were not due to *race*, but— before 1940— they were at least as far below the national average IQ of 100 as were the IQs of black children. These results seem consistent with what geographer Ellen Churchill Semple said, back in 1911, that human advancement "slackens its pace" in the foothills and "comes to a halt" in the mountains.[68] Other studies of life in isolated mountain and foothill communities around the world show similar patterns of both poverty and lagging human development.[69]

Later years would bring additional evidence incompatible with genetic determinism. A 1976 study showed that black orphans raised by white families had significantly higher average IQs than other black children, and IQs slightly above the national average.[70] It so happens that one of the first notable black scientists— George Washington Carver, in the early twentieth century— was an orphan raised by a white family.[71]

Genetic determinism in the early twentieth century was by no means simply an issue about black and white Americans. The belief that blacks were genetically inferior was already so widely accepted that most of the genetic determinism literature of that era focused on arguing that people from Eastern Europe and Southern Europe were genetically inferior to people from Western Europe and Northern Europe. This was a major issue in that era, because large-scale emigration from Europe had changed in its origins from predominantly Western Europe and Northern Europe in earlier times to predominantly Eastern Europe and Southern Europe, beginning in the last two decades of the nineteenth century.

Among the massive new wave of immigrants were Eastern European Jews. A leading mental test authority in that era, Carl Brigham— creator of the Scholastic Aptitude Test (SAT)— said that the Army mental test results tended to "disprove the popular belief that the Jew is highly intelligent."[72] Another mental test authority, H.H. Goddard, who tested children of these Eastern European and Southern European immigrants at the Ellis Island immigrant receiving facility, declared that "These people cannot deal with abstractions."[73]

Prominent economist of that era Francis A. Walker described immigrants from Eastern Europe and Southern Europe as "beaten men from beaten races"[74]— a "foul and stagnant pool of population in Europe," originating in places where "no breath of intellectual life has stirred for ages."[75]

Professor Edward A. Ross, an official of the American Economic Association and President of the American Sociological Association, coined the term "race suicide" to describe the prospect of a demographic replacement over time of the Western Europeans and Northern Europeans as the majority of the American population by Eastern Europeans and Southern Europeans, because both these latter groups had a higher birthrate.[76] He called these new immigrants "oxlike men," and descendants of backward peoples, whose very physical appearance "proclaims inferiority of type."[77]

Professor Ross lamented an "unanticipated result" of widespread access to medical advances— namely, "the brightening of the survival prospect of the ignorant, the stupid, the careless and the very poor."[78]

Ross was the author of more than two dozen books, with large sales.[79] The introduction to one of his books included a letter of fulsome praise from Theodore Roosevelt.[80] Among Professor Ross' academic colleagues was Roscoe Pound, who later became dean of the Harvard law school. Professor Pound credited Professor Ross with setting him "in the path the world is moving in."[81] This sense of mission, and a history-is-on-our-side assumption, marked Roscoe Pound's influential writings over a long career, as he promoted judicial activism to free government from Constitutional restrictions, leaving judges with a more expansive role to play in promoting Progressive social policies.[82]

The people who led the crusade for genetic determinism in the early twentieth century were *not* ill-educated, lower-class people. They included some of the most intellectually prominent people of that era, on both sides of the Atlantic.

These included the founders of such scholarly organizations as the American Economic Association[83] and the American Sociological Association,[84] a president of Stanford University and a president of MIT,[85] as well as renowned professors at leading universities across the United States.[86] In England, John Maynard Keynes was one of the founders of the eugenics society at Cambridge University.[87] Most of these intellectuals were on the political left in both countries.[88] But there were also some conservatives, including Winston Churchill and Neville Chamberlain.[89]

There were hundreds of courses on eugenics in colleges and universities across the United States,[90] just as there are similarly ideological courses on college and university campuses across the country today, promoting very different ideologies as regards race, but with a very similar sense of mission, and a very similar intolerance toward those who do not share their ideology or their mission.

"Eugenics" was a term coined by Sir Francis Galton, to describe an agenda to reduce or prevent the survival of people considered genetically inferior. He said, "there exists a sentiment, for the most part quite unreasonable, against the gradual extinction of an inferior race."[91] Professor Richard T. Ely, one of the founders of the American Economic Association, said of the people he considered genetically inferior: "We must give to the most hopeless classes left behind in our social progress custodial care with the highest possible development and with segregation of sexes and confinement to prevent reproduction."[92]

Other contemporary academics of great distinction expressed very similar views. Professor Irving Fisher of Yale, the leading American monetary economist of his day, advocated the prevention of the "breeding of the worst" by "isolation in public institutions and in some cases by surgical operation."[93] Professor Henry Rogers Seager, of Columbia University, likewise said that "we must courageously cut off lines of heredity that have been proved to be undesirable," even if that requires "isolation or sterilization."[94]

Prominent Harvard professor of economics Frank Taussig said of a variety of people he considered inferior, that if it were not feasible to "chloroform them once and for all," then "at least they can be segregated, shut up in refuges and asylums, and prevented from propagating their kind."[95]

The casual ease with which leading scholars of their time could advocate imprisoning people for life, who had committed no crime, and depriving them of a normal life, is a painfully sobering reminder of what can happen when an idea or a vision becomes a heady dogma that overwhelms all other considerations. A widely read book of that era, *The Passing of the Great Race* by Madison Grant, declared that "race lies at the base of all the manifestation of modern society"[96] and deplored "a sentimental belief in the sanctity of human life," when that is used "to prevent both the elimination of defective infants and the sterilization of such adults as are themselves of no value to the community."[97]

This book was translated into other languages, including German, and Hitler called it his "Bible."[98]

The early twentieth-century Progressives were by no means Nazis. They took pride in advocating a wide range of policies for social betterment, very similar to the kinds of policies that would be advocated by other Progressives in the later years of the twentieth century, and on into our own times.

Prominent economist Richard T. Ely, for example, rejected free-market economics because he saw government power as something to be applied "to the amelioration of the conditions under which people live or work." Far from seeing government power as a threat to freedom, he said, "regulation by the power of the state of these industrial and other social relations existing among men is a condition of freedom."[99] He favored "public ownership" of municipal utilities, highways and railroads— and declared that "labor unions should be legally encouraged in their efforts for shorter hours and higher wages" and that "inheritance and income taxes should be generally extended."[100] Eugenics was to him just another social benefit he wanted provided by government.

Professor Ely was clearly a man of the left, and has been called "the father of institutional economics"[101]— a branch of economics long noted for its opposition to free-market economics. One of Ely's students— John R. Commons— became a leading institutional economist at the University of Wisconsin. Professor Commons rejected free-market competition because "competition has no respect for the superior races," so that "the race with lowest necessities displaces others."[102]

Among Ely's other students was the iconic Progressive President of the United States, Woodrow Wilson.[103] President Wilson too saw some races as inferior. He approved of the annexation of Puerto Rico by President William McKinley before him, saying of those annexed, "they are children and we are men in these deep matters of government and justice."[104] Wilson's own administration segregated black employees of federal agencies in Washington,[105] and he showed the movie, "Birth of A Nation"— glorifying the Ku Klux Klan— in the White House to invited guests.[106]

Like other Progressives of his time and later times, Woodrow Wilson saw no dangers to freedom in an expansion of government power— whether through the creation of new federal agencies like the Federal Trade Commission and the Federal Reserve System during his own administration,[107] or through the appointment of federal judges who would "interpret" the Constitution so as to loosen what President Wilson regarded as excessive restriction on the powers of government.[108]

In his book *The New Freedom*, Woodrow Wilson arbitrarily defined government benefits as a new form of freedom,[109] thereby verbally finessing aside concerns about expanding powers of government being a threat to people's freedom. This redefinition of freedom has persisted among various later advocates of expanding welfare state powers, on into the twenty-first century.[110]

Among other prominent scholars of the early Progressive era who were clearly on the political left, along with advocating eugenics, was the already mentioned Professor Edward A. Ross, who was regarded as one of the founders of the profession of sociology in the United States. Professor Ross referred to "us liberals" as people who speak up "for public interests against powerful selfish private interests," and denounced those who disagreed with his views as unworthy "kept" spokesmen for special interests, a "mercenary corps" as contrasted with "us champions of the social welfare."[111]

In their own minds, at least, these early twentieth-century Progressives were advocating social justice— and Roscoe Pound used that specific phrase.[112] There is no need to question Ross' sincerity, as he questioned others' sincerity. People can be very sincere when presupposing their own superiority.

Madison Grant, whose book Hitler called his "Bible," was likewise a staunch Progressive of the early twentieth century. While not an academic scholar, neither was he an ignorant redneck. He was from a wealthy family in New York, and he was educated at Yale and the Columbia University law school. He was an activist in Progressive causes, such as conservation, preserving endangered species, municipal reform and the creation of national parks.[113] He was welcomed into an exclusive social club established by Theodore Roosevelt,[114] and during the 1920s he exchanged friendly letters with Franklin D. Roosevelt, addressing him in these letters as "My dear Frank," while FDR reciprocated by addressing him as "My dear Madison."[115]

In short, the Progressives of the early twentieth century shared more than a name with Progressives of a later era, extending on into our own times. While these different generations of Progressives reached opposite conclusions on the reasons for racial differences in economic and social outcomes, they shared very similar views on the role of government in general and judges in particular. They also had similar practices in dealing with empirical evidence. Both remained largely impervious to evidence or conclusions contrary to their own beliefs.

In addressing one of the central issues in early twentieth-century America— the massive increase in immigration from Eastern Europe and Southern Europe that began in the 1880s— the Progressives went beyond claiming that the current generation of immigrants was less productive or less advanced than the previous generations from Western Europe and Northern Europe. The Progressives' claim was that Eastern Europeans and Southern Europeans were inherently, genetically— and therefore permanently— inferior, whether in the past or the future.

Ironically, the Western civilization that all these Europeans shared originated, thousands of years earlier, in Southern Europe— specifically in ancient Greece, located in the eastern Mediterranean. The very words that genetic determinists wrote were written in letters created in Southern Europe by the Romans. In those ancient times, it was the Southern Europeans who were more advanced. In the ancient days of the Roman Empire, Cicero warned his fellow Romans not to buy British slaves, because they were so hard to teach.[116] It is difficult to see how it could have been otherwise, when someone from an illiterate tribal people in ancient Britain was brought in bondage to a highly complex and sophisticated civilization like that in ancient Rome.

As for the claim that Southern European and Eastern European immigrant children tested at Ellis Island "cannot deal with abstractions,"[117] that can hardly be taken as proof of a *genetic* inability of people from these regions to deal with abstractions. The ancient Greeks did not simply learn mathematics. They were among the *creators* of mathematics— Euclid in geometry and Pythagoras in trigonometry.

Nor need we believe that there was some *biological* superiority of the ancient Greeks in southeastern Europe. A series of geographic treatises on the history of Europe's socioeconomic development by Professor N.J.G. Pounds offered a very different explanation of why the earliest developments of Western civilization began where they did:

> Most of the significant advances in man's material culture, like agriculture and the smelting of metals, had been made in the Middle East and had entered Europe through the Balkan peninsula. From here they had been diffused northwestward to central Europe and then to western.[118]

World leadership in various fundamental advances of human beings has changed hands repeatedly over the thousands of years of recorded history. That Western Europe and Northern Europe were more advanced in some respects than Eastern Europe and Southern Europe in the early twentieth century was no mandate for genetic determinists to eternalize that relationship to the past and the future.

Among peoples of various races, in countries around the world, those groups that score low on mental tests typically score lowest on abstract questions.[119] This hardly seems surprising, since abstractions do not play major roles in all people's lives— especially not among low-income, working-class people, who predominated among the immigrants from Southern Europe and Eastern Europe, who were tested at Ellis Island.

The story was very different among the ancient Greek elites, whose achievements included not only mathematics but also philosophy, literature and architecture. The ancient Greeks created magnificent buildings in the Acropolis that have served as models for iconic buildings in many other countries, thousands of years later. The Capitol building in the United States, and the Supreme Court building across the street from the Capitol, are examples. Anyone who has seen both the Lincoln Memorial in Washington and the Parthenon built in ancient Athens can hardly fail to notice the resemblance. The ancient Greeks also created exquisite statues and busts of human beings that people still marvel at and admire in museums in various countries today.

By contrast, the primitive structures and crude attempts at representing human likenesses, by those ancient Britons who were contemporaries of the ancient Greeks, inspire no such admiration or imitation. Names of ancient Greek thinkers like Socrates, Plato, Aristotle, Euclid and Pythagoras still resonate today. But there is not a single Briton from those same ancient times whose name can be found in the pages of history.[120]

Nevertheless, in the eighteenth and nineteenth centuries A.D., Britons led the world into the industrial revolution. Moreover, the scientific breakthroughs of Britons in the centuries preceding the industrial revolution— including the scientific achievements of Sir Isaac Newton, who was also one of the creators of calculus— dwarf anything produced among Britain's nineteenth-century Greek contemporaries. The British Empire of the nineteenth century included one-fourth of the land area of the Earth and one-fourth of all the human beings on the planet. A twentieth-century Italian author raised the question: "How, in the first place, did a peripheral island rise from primitive squalor to world domination?"[121]

These undisputed facts of history argue against genetic determinism, when peoples in different parts of Europe were clearly more advanced in different centuries. Such radical changes over millennia suggest reciprocal inequalities on a grand scale, from very different historical epochs.

Some people with a non-judgmental philosophy today might refuse to say that the capabilities of either Greeks or Britons were superior. But that is just a verbal evasion of the plain reality that each had superior capabilities to the other in different epochs. What such reversals of relative capabilities from one epoch to another calls into question is whether these different capabilities were *genetic*.

To honestly admit the reality of vast differences in specific capabilities of different peoples, at different times and in different places, is no capitulation to genetic determinism. Nor are comparisons between different groups of Europeans the only evidence against a genetic explanation. A thousand years ago, the Chinese were more advanced than Europeans in many endeavors.[122] But, several centuries later, their positions were reversed— and there is no evidence that the genetic makeup of either the Chinese or the Europeans had changed.

Moreover, there have been similarly large disparities *within* different segments of the same race. In 1994, for example, the millions of overseas Chinese produced as much wealth as the billion people in China.[123] Here the race was the same, but the production of wealth per capita was radically different. A similar pattern can also be found in the United States today, when several of the very poorest counties in the country have overwhelmingly white populations, with median household incomes lower than the median household incomes of black Americans.[124] No one has gone into those counties and exploited those people. They have simply not produced as much.

The genetic determinists of the early Progressive era took a remarkably narrow sample of the evidence available to them. The history of ancient Greece and Rome was already well-known as the origins of Western civilization, and places far in advance of the rest of Europe in ancient times. Whatever the relative positions of different regions of Europe during the Progressive era, to see their positions at that time as genetically determined implied that these positions were permanent, for both the future and the past. But readily available evidence about the past said otherwise.

Even the purely contemporary evidence used during the early Progressive era was by no means unambiguous. Answering questions in one section of the Army mental tests required knowing such information as the color of sapphires, the location of Cornell University, the profession of Alfred Noyes and the city in which the Pierce Arrow automobile was manufactured.[125] Why black Americans, or recent immigrants to the United States, would be expected to have such information is a puzzle. Why such information would be considered a measure of anyone's innate intelligence is a bigger puzzle.

Not all the questions on the Army mental tests were as dubious as these. But, for someone who was not quite up to par in answering more valid questions, to have his imprisonment or his freedom depend on whether he had such miscellaneous information seems grotesque.

Mental test pioneer Carl Brigham asserted in 1923 that the Army mental tests provided an "inventory" of "mental capacity" with "a scientific basis."[126] This was neither the first nor the last time when the word "scientific" was invoked, without either the procedures or the precision of science. Brigham was, however, one of the few who later recanted. Writing in 1930, he belatedly pointed out that many of the immigrant men tested by the Army were raised in homes where the language spoken was not English. He candidly declared that his previous conclusions were— in his own words— "without foundation."[127]

How many of today's totally convinced people, with opposite convictions, will be able to later follow in Carl Brigham's footsteps, only the future can tell.

With the passing years, more and more evidence accumulated that undermined the conclusions of Progressive-era genetic determinists. For example, Jews who had scored low on the 1917 Army mental tests began to score above the national average on various IQ tests and college admissions tests,[128] as they became a more English-speaking group. This and other evidence, such as the IQs of black orphans raised by white families,[129] undermined the central premise of genetic determinism— its rationale for urging drastic steps to prevent some races from reproducing, on the assumption that such races' higher birthrates would lead to a decline in the nation's IQ over time.

A decisive blow was dealt to that argument by the later research of Professor James R. Flynn, an American expatriate in New Zealand. His research showed that, in more than a dozen countries around the world, the average performance on IQ tests *rose* substantially— by a standard deviation or more— in a generation or two.[130]

This trend had been going on for years, before Professor Flynn's research brought it to light. The reason it was not obvious to others before him was that IQ test results were repeatedly renormed, in order to maintain the average number of questions answered correctly at its definitional level of 100.[131] As more people answered more IQ test questions correctly over the years, an IQ of 100 now represented correctly answering more questions than before. Because Professor Flynn went back to the original raw scores on IQ test questions answered correctly, these rising performances on IQ tests were brought to light.[132]

Although the black IQ average, for example, remained more or less constant at about 85 for years, this constancy concealed the fact that blacks, like others, were answering more IQ test questions correctly than in the past. The number of questions that blacks answered correctly on IQ tests in 2002 would have given them an average IQ of 104 by the norms used in 1947–1948. This was slightly higher than the average performance of Americans in general during the earlier period.[133]

In short, the performances of blacks on IQ tests had risen significantly over time, just as the performances of other people in the United States and in other countries had risen, even though the renorming of IQ tests concealed these changes. Later data published by Charles Murray in 2021 showed that the mean black IQ was now 91,[134] up from the usual 85 in earlier times. This meant that black improvement on IQ tests had not simply kept pace with other people's improvement but had improved somewhat more.

The devastating effect of Professor Flynn's research was that it destroyed the central rationale for the conclusions of early twentieth-century, Progressive-era genetic determinists, who had proclaimed an urgent necessity to prevent people with lower IQs from reproducing, on the assumption that such people were genetically incapable of reaching the same average intellectual level that was then current. Therefore, on that assumption, the intelligence of the nation as a whole would decline over time. But, even if we assume, for the sake of argument, that IQ test results are a perfect measure of intelligence, the factual evidence is that people in multiple countries were correctly answering *more* IQ test questions in later years, not fewer.

Something else was implicit in the genetic determinism of early twentieth-century Progressivism— namely, that there was a genetically determined *ceiling* on the intelligence of some groups, making it imperative that they be prevented from reproducing. As late as 1944, Gunnar Myrdal reported, in his path-breaking book *An American Dilemma,* that belief in a low ceiling on black intelligence was common among white Americans at that time.[135]

Nevertheless, just one generation later, even the leading academic scholar researching the effect of genes on IQ— Professor Arthur R. Jensen, of the University of California at Berkeley— repudiated the IQ ceiling conclusion, and asked "why should anyone be surprised to find that there are Negro children having IQs of 115 or higher, or that they should be concentrated in the affluent integrated neighborhood in Los Angeles?"[136]

With the implicit assumption of a low IQ ceiling by the early Progressive-era genetic determinists now gone, and the falling IQ test performances expected now contradicted by widespread *rises* in performances on IQ tests in later generations, as discovered by Professor Flynn's research,[137] that era is a chapter in human history now mercifully closed— though not before it provided a rationale for *genocide*. Its enduring significance for our era is as a painfully urgent warning against intolerant ideological stampedes, even when these stampedes are led by leading scholars and intellectuals, and spread by a wide range of institutions.

Later Progressivism

In the later decades of the twentieth century, and on into the twenty-first century, latter-day Progressives substituted racial discrimination for genes as the automatic explanation of group differences in economic and social outcomes. Mental tests— once exalted as an embodiment of "science," supposedly proving genetic determinism— were now automatically dismissed as biased, when SAT and ACT college admissions tests produced results that conflicted with the new social justice agenda of imposed demographic representation of various social groups in various institutions and endeavors.

In this new Progressive era, statistical disparities between blacks and whites, in any endeavor, have usually been sufficient to produce a conclusion that racial discrimination was the reason. Often there are also statistical data on Asian Americans in these same endeavors. But these Asian American data are almost invariably omitted, not only by the media, but even by academic scholars in elite universities. Such data would often present a serious challenge to the conclusions reached by latter-day Progressives.

In the job market, for example, it has often been said that blacks are "the last hired and the first fired," when there are downturns in the economy. Black employees may in fact be terminated during an economic downturn, sooner or to a greater extent than white employees.

But data also show that white employees are often let go before Asian American employees.[138] Can this be attributed to racial discrimination against whites, by employers who were usually white themselves? Are we to accept statistical data as evidence when these data fit existing preconceptions, but not accept such data when they go counter to those same preconceptions?

Or are we to be spared such problems by those who simply omit facts that go against their vision or agenda?

One of the major factors in the housing boom and bust, which produced an economic crisis in the United States, early in the twenty-first century, was a widespread belief that there was rampant racial discrimination by banks and other lending institutions against blacks applying for mortgage loans. Various statistics from a number of sources showed that, although most black and white applicants for conventional mortgage loans were approved, black applicants were turned down at a higher rate than white applicants for the same loans. What was almost universally omitted were statistical data showing that whites were turned down for those same loans more often than Asian Americans.[139]

Nor was there any great mystery as to why this was so. The average credit rating of whites was higher than the average credit rating of blacks— and the average credit rating of Asian Americans was higher than the average credit rating of whites.[140] Nor was this the only economically relevant difference.[141]

Nevertheless, there were outraged demands in the media, in academia and in politics that the government should "do something" about racial discrimination by banks and other mortgage lenders. The government responded by doing many things. The net result was that it forced mortgage lenders to lower their lending standards.[142] This made mortgage loans so risky that many people, including the author of this book, warned that the housing market could "collapse like a house of cards."[143] When it did, the whole economy collapsed.[144] Low-income blacks were among those who suffered.

The same question can be raised about mortgage approval patterns as the question about hiring and firing in the job market. Were predominantly white mortgage lenders discriminating against white applicants? If that seems highly unlikely, it is also unlikely that black-owned banks were discriminating against black mortgage loan applicants. Yet black applicants for mortgage loans were turned down at an even higher rate by a black-owned bank.[145]

It has been much the same story with student discipline in the public schools. Statistics show that black males have been disciplined for misbehavior more often than white males. Because of the prevailing preconception that the behavior of different groups themselves cannot be different, this automatically became another example of racial discrimination— and literally a federal issue. A joint declaration from the U.S. Department of Education and the U.S. Department of Justice warned public school officials that they wanted what they characterized as a racially discriminatory pattern ended.[146]

Statistical data from a landmark study of American education— *No Excuses: Closing the Racial Gap in Learning* by Abigail Thernstrom and Stephan Thernstrom— showed that black students were disciplined two-and-a-half times as often as white students, *who were disciplined twice as often as Asian students.*[147] Were the predominantly white teachers biased against white students? Nor was the disciplining of black students correlated with whether the teachers involved were black or white.[148]

Although we may analyze all these statistics by race, that does not necessarily mean that the employers, lenders or teachers made their decisions on the basis of race. If black, white and Asian employees had different distributions of jobs, or were distributed differently at different levels in the same occupations, then decisions as to which kinds of jobs— or job performances— were expendable during an economic downturn could result in the racial disparities seen.

Banking officials who decided whose mortgage applications to accept or reject are unlikely to have actually seen the applicants themselves. These applicants would more likely be interviewed by lower-level bank employees. These employees would then pass the income and other data— including individual credit ratings— on to higher officials, who would then either approve or disapprove the applications. In the public schools, teachers would obviously see the students whose misbehavior they reported, but the fact that black and white teachers made similar reports, suggests that race was not likely to be the key factor in this case either.

Perhaps the point in American history when there was the widest consensus on racial issues, across racial lines, was the occasion of the historic speech by Martin Luther King at the Lincoln Memorial in 1963. That was when he said that his dream was of a world where people "will not be judged by the color of their skin but by the content of their character."[149] His message was equal opportunity for individuals, regardless of race. But that agenda, and the wide consensus it had, began eroding in the years that followed. The goal changed from equal opportunity for individuals, regardless of race, to equal outcomes for groups, whether these groups were defined by race, sex or otherwise.

What now rose to dominance was the social justice agenda, which included equalized outcomes in the present and reparations for the past. This new agenda drew on history, or on myths presented as history, as well as assertions presented as facts— the latter in a spirit reminiscent of the certitude and heedlessness of evidence in the genetic determinism era.

Chapter 3

CHESS PIECES FALLACIES

In much of the social justice literature, including Professor John Rawls' classic *A Theory of Justice*, various policies have been recommended, on grounds of their desirability from a moral standpoint— but often with little or no attention to the practical question of whether those policies could in fact be carried out and produce the end results desired. In a number of places, for example, Rawls referred to things that "society" should "arrange"[1]— but without specifying either the instrumentalities or the feasibilities of those arrangements.

It is hard to imagine what institution could take on such a gigantic task, other than government. That in turn raises questions about the dangers of putting more power in the hands of politicians who run the government. The innocent-sounding word "arrange" cannot be allowed to obscure those dangers. Interior decorators *arrange*. Governments *compel*. It is not a subtle distinction.

Governments must compel some things, ranging from traffic laws to laws against murder. But that does not mean that there are no dangers to be considered when expanding government compulsion for whatever seems desirable. That would mean destroying everyone's freedom for the sake of whatever crusade has caught the fancy of some influential segment of the population.

Rawls' approach has by no means been unique to Rawls, or even to modern times. Back in the eighteenth century, there were people with similar ideas. Adam Smith expressed his opposition to such people, and to the very presumption of some doctrinaire theorist— a "man of system," as he put it— who "seems to imagine that he can arrange the different members of a great society with as much ease as the hand arranges the different pieces upon a chess-board."[2]

The exaltation of *desirability* and neglect of *feasibility*, which Adam Smith criticized, is today still a major ingredient in the fundamental fallacies of the social justice vision. Its implications extend to a wide variety of issues, ranging from the redistribution of wealth to the interpretation of income statistics.

The confiscation and redistribution of wealth— whether on a moderate or a comprehensive scale— is at the heart of the social justice agenda. While social justice advocates stress what they see as the desirability of such policies, the feasibility of those policies tends to receive far less attention, and the consequences of trying and failing often receive virtually no attention.

There is no question that governments, or even local looters, can redistribute wealth to some extent. But the larger issue is whether the actual effects of attempting more comprehensive and enduring confiscation and redistribution policies are likely to be successful or counterproductive. Leaving moral issues aside for the moment, these are ultimately factual questions, for which we must seek answers in the realm of empirical evidence, rather than in theories or rhetoric.

REDISTRIBUTION OF WEALTH

Politically attractive as confiscation and redistribution of the wealth of "the rich" might seem, the extent to which it can actually be carried out in practice depends on the extent to which "the rich" are conceived as being like inert pieces on a chessboard. To the extent that "the rich" can foresee and react to redistributive policies, the actual consequences can be very different from what was intended.

In an absolute monarchy or a totalitarian dictatorship, a mass confiscation of wealth can be suddenly imposed without warning on the "millionaires and billionaires" so often cited as targets of confiscation. But, in a country with a democratically elected government, confiscatory taxation or other forms of confiscation must first be publicly proposed, and then develop sufficient political support over time among the voters, before being actually imposed by law. If "millionaires and billionaires" are not oblivious to all this, there is little chance that they will not know about the impending confiscation and redistribution before it happens. Nor can we assume that they will simply wait passively to be sheared like sheep.

Among the more obvious options available to "the rich"— when they are forewarned of large-scale confiscations of their wealth— include (1) investing their wealth in tax-exempt securities, (2) sending their wealth beyond the taxing jurisdiction, or (3) moving themselves personally beyond the taxing jurisdiction.

In the United States, the taxing jurisdiction can be a city, a state or the federal government. The various ways of sheltering wealth from taxation may have some costs to "the rich" and, where their wealth is embodied in immovable assets such as steel mills or chains of stores, there may be little they can do to escape confiscation of these particular forms of wealth. But, for liquid assets in today's globalized economies around the world, vast sums of money can be transferred electronically from country to country, with the click of a computer mouse.

This means that the actual consequences of raising tax rates on "the rich" in a given jurisdiction is a factual question. The outcome is not necessarily predictable, and the potential consequences may or may not make the planned confiscation feasible. Raising the tax *rate* X percent does not guarantee that the tax *revenue* will also rise X percent— or will even rise at all. When we turn from theories and rhetoric to the facts of history, we can put both the explicit and the implicit assumptions of the social justice vision to the test.

History

Back in the eighteenth century, Britain's imposition of a new tax on its American colonies played a major role in setting off a chain of events that led ultimately to those colonies declaring their independence, and becoming the United States of America. Edmund Burke pointed out at the time, in the British Parliament: "Your scheme yields no revenue; it yields nothing but discontent, disorder, disobedience. . ."[3]

Americans were not just inert pieces on the great chessboard of the British Empire. American independence deprived Britain not only of revenue from the new taxes they imposed, but also deprived the British of revenue from the other taxes they had already been collecting from the American colonies. This was by no means the only time when an increase in the official rate of taxation led to a *reduction* in the tax revenues actually collected.

Tax Rates versus Tax Revenues

Centuries later, similar withdrawals from taxing jurisdictions took place within the United States. The state of Maryland, for example, anticipated collecting more than $100 million in additional tax revenues, by increasing the tax rate on people whose incomes were a million dollars a year or more. But, by the time the new tax rate took effect in 2008, the number of such people living in Maryland had declined from nearly 8,000 to fewer than 6,000. The tax revenues, which had been anticipated to rise by more than $100 million, actually *fell* instead by more than $200 million.[4]

Likewise, when Oregon raised its income tax rate in 2009 on people earning $250,000 a year or more, its income tax revenues also *fell* instead of rising.[5] Americans were still not inert chess pieces.

None of this has been peculiar to Americans, however. Similar things have happened when other countries raised— or even threatened to raise— tax rates substantially on high incomes, in the expectation that this would automatically bring in more tax revenue, which it may or may not do. When such plans were advanced in Britain, for example, the *Wall Street Journal* reported:

> A stream of hedge-fund managers and other financial-services professionals are quitting the U.K., following plans to raise top personal tax rates to 51%....Lawyers estimate hedge funds managing close to $15 billion have moved to Switzerland in the past year, with more possibly to come.[6]

Conversely, a *reduction* in tax rates does not automatically result in a reduction in tax revenues. People are not inert chess pieces in either case. Just as higher tax rates can repel people, businesses and investments, lower tax rates can attract them. In Iceland, as the corporate tax rate was gradually reduced from 45 percent to 18 percent between 1991 and 2001, tax revenues tripled.[7]

In the United States, tax-exempt securities provide an obvious way for high-income people to avoid paying high tax rates. As the federal income tax rate rose sharply during the Woodrow Wilson administration, the number of people reporting taxable incomes of $300,000 or more declined from well over a thousand in 1916 to less than three hundred in 1921. The federal income tax rate on the highest incomes in 1920 was 73 percent.[8] By 1928, the highest income tax rate had been reduced to 25 percent. Between those two years, the total amount of income tax revenue collected *increased*, and the proportion of all income taxes collected from people earning a million dollars or more per year also *increased*, from less than 5 percent in 1920 to 15.9 percent in 1928.[9]

In advocating these tax rate reductions in the 1920s, Secretary of the Treasury Andrew Mellon pointed out that the rich had vast sums of money invested in tax-exempt securities.[10] These securities paid a lower rate of return than other securities that were subject to taxation. Investing in tax-exempt securities, despite their lower rate of return, made sense when the top tax rate was 73 percent. But, at a top tax rate of 25 percent, it made sense for many high-income people to shift their investments to other securities that paid a higher rate of return, even though that return was subject to taxation.

High-income people, not being inert chess pieces, figured this out. So the federal government collected more tax revenue from them at the lower tax rate, because 25 percent of something is larger than 73 percent of nothing.

Both Secretary of the Treasury Andrew Mellon and President Calvin Coolidge said beforehand that a reduction of the tax *rate* would increase the tax *revenue*,[11] as it did, and bring in more tax revenue from high-income people. Secretary Mellon had also complained that tax-exempt securities had created a situation that was "repugnant" in a democracy— namely, that there was, in effect, "a class in the community which cannot be reached for tax purposes."[12] Failing to get Congress to take steps to end tax-exempt securities,[13] Mellon was at least able to get higher income people to pay a larger share of the income taxes by other means.

Nevertheless, Mellon's arguments for reducing the top tax rate were denounced as "tax cuts for the rich," as similar plans for similar reasons have been denounced ever since.[14]

For some— including distinguished professors at elite universities— the implicit assumption that tax *revenues* automatically move in the same direction as tax *rates* seems impervious to factual evidence. But such evidence is readily available on the Internet from the official records of the Internal Revenue Service.[15] Nevertheless, the chess pieces fallacy remains largely unchallenged, so social justice advocates can continue to advocate higher tax rates on the rich, on the basis of its *desirability* from their perspective, without regard to questions as to its *feasibility* as a revenue-collection mechanism.

In politics, highly expensive proposals to have the government provide various benefits "free" to everyone can be very appealing to some voters, when the additional costs to the government are said to be paid for by collecting higher tax revenues from "millionaires and billionaires," whether or not this actually turns out to be true. Such an outcome might seem desirable to some voters, from a social justice perspective, but *desirability* does not preclude questions of *feasibility*.

In politics, the goal is not truth but votes. If most voters believe what is said, that rhetoric is a success, as far as politicians are concerned. But, from the standpoint of the public, the claim that the cost of government giveaways will be paid for by taxes collected from "millionaires and billionaires" is a proposition that very much requires empirical examination, since "millionaires and billionaires" are not always cooperative.

People who imagine that the benefits they receive "free" from government will be paid for by others may discover that they themselves end up paying for those benefits, as a result of inflation.

The Inflation "Tax"

Just as tax rates on paper are not necessarily collected, so things that are *not* taxes can have the same effect as taxes. Inflation is one of those things.

When tax revenues to pay for "free" benefits given to various groups fail to cover the expenses of those benefits, the government can get additional money needed to cover the deficit by issuing more government bonds and selling them. To the extent that these bonds are purchased in the market, the cost is passed on, with interest added, to taxpayers in the future. But, if not enough of these bonds are bought in the market to cover the remaining deficit, these bonds can be purchased by the Federal Reserve System, a federal government agency legally authorized to create money. Then, as this additional money goes into circulation, the result is inflation.

The net result of inflationary price increases is that *everyone's money*— regardless of their income— loses some of its value. It is the same as if a tax had been imposed on everybody, from the poorest to the richest, and with everyone paying the same tax rate on their money as "millionaires and billionaires" pay. But a tax on money is *not* a tax on tangible assets, such as factories or real estate— which increase in market value during an inflation. The net result of all this is that an inflation "tax" can take a higher percentage of the assets of the poorest people, whose money is likely to be a higher percentage of their total assets, because they are less likely to own factories, real estate and other tangible assets that rise in market value during an inflation.

In short, an inflation "tax" is likely to be a *regressive* tax, paid whenever buying groceries, gasoline or other consumer goods at higher prices. The illusion of getting "free" benefits from the government may be maintained, so long as the recipients do not see the connection between the higher prices they end up paying for what they buy, after the government gives them "free" things.

The biggest beneficiaries of this situation are likely to be politicians, who can attract voters by offering them "free" benefits— "as a right, not a privilege"— which the voters end up paying for in a roundabout way, through inflationary price increases on the things they buy.

Politicians cover their tracks by calling the key mechanism— the Federal Reserve's creation of money to buy government bonds— by the obscure insider phrase, "quantitative easing," instead of saying in plain English that the government is producing more of its own money, in order to pay for the things it is giving away "free." Sometimes a technical-sounding term— "QE2"— is used, to designate a second round of creating money. That sounds so much more impressive than simply saying "producing more money for politicians to spend."

CHESS PIECES AND PRICE CONTROLS

Just as people's behavior changes when governments change tax rates, so their behavior changes when governments change the terms of other transactions. This is one of the most basic principles of economics. It has been known for centuries by economists, and even by others before there was any such occupation as an economist.[16] But what has been known by some has not been known by all, so governments have been setting prices on various goods and services by law, for thousands of years— going back to Roman times, and even to ancient Babylon before that.[17]

Reactions to Price Controls

The people subject to price-setting laws have seldom remained passive, as if they were inert chess pieces. How many governments understood this before they passed such laws is unknown. But what is known is that a President of the United States— Richard Nixon— who was fully aware of the adverse economic consequences of price controls, imposed those controls anyway. His response to criticism of that decision by economist Milton Friedman was: "I don't give a good goddamn *what* Milton Friedman says. He's not running for re-election."[18] President Nixon was in fact re-elected, by a larger majority than that which first put him in the White House.

As for the economic consequences of the price controls, they were what such consequences have been in other places and times, going back for centuries. At prices set by government below the level set by supply and demand, the amount demanded by consumers went up— because of the artificially lower prices— and the amount produced by producers went down, also because of those same artificially lower prices. Neither consumers nor producers were inert chess pieces. The net result was that there were widespread shortages of food, gasoline and numerous other things. But these consequences became widely apparent only *after* the election.[19]

None of this was peculiar to the United States. When the government of the African nation of Zimbabwe decreed drastic cutbacks in prices to deal with runaway inflation in 2007, the *New York Times* reported that citizens of Zimbabwe "greeted the price cuts with a euphoric— and short-lived— shopping spree." But, as in the United States, this increase in the amount consumers demanded was accompanied by a *decrease* in the amount that producers supplied:

> Bread, sugar and cornmeal, staples of every Zimbabwean's diet, have vanished... Meat is virtually nonexistent, even for members of the middle class who have money to buy it on the black market... Hospital patients are dying for lack of basic medical supplies.[20]

The people in Africa were not inert chess pieces, any more than people in Europe or America.

Many studies of many forms of price controls, in countries around the world, have revealed very similar patterns.[21] This has led some people to ask: "Why don't politicians learn from their mistakes?" Politicians *do* learn. They learn what is politically effective, and what they do is *not* a mistake politically, despite how disastrous such policies may turn out to be for the country. What can be a mistake politically is to assume that particular ideals— including social justice— can be something that society can just "arrange," through government, without considering the particular patterns of incentives and constraints inherent in the institution of government.

Minimum Wage Laws

Not all price control laws force prices down. Some price control laws force prices up. In these latter cases, producers produce more, because of the higher prices, but consumers buy less. Again, people are not inert chess pieces in either case. While price control laws that force prices down tend to create shortages, price control laws that force prices up tend to create unsalable surpluses.

Rent control laws are examples of the former, and such laws have created housing shortages in cities around the world.[22] Agricultural price support programs in the United States are an example of the latter, and they lead to farmers growing larger crops than the consumers will buy, at the artificially higher prices. The unsalable surpluses have led to expensive government programs to buy this surplus output— and store it, while figuring out how to dispose of it and limit future production. These costs run into many billions of dollars of the taxpayers' money.

A special form of price control to force prices up are minimum wage laws, often supported by people with a social justice vision.

Minimum wage laws are among the many government policies widely believed to benefit the poor, by preventing them from making decisions for themselves that surrogate decision-makers regard as being not as good as what the surrogates can impose through the power of government.

Traditional basic economics, however, says that people tend to purchase less at a higher price. If so, then employers— not being inert chess pieces— tend to hire less labor at a higher price, imposed by minimum wage laws, than they would hire at a lower price, based on supply and demand. Here the unsalable surplus is called unemployment.

Although minimum wage rates are usually set by law at a level lower than what the average worker makes, these laws nevertheless tend to set wage rates *higher* than what an unskilled beginner would earn by supply and demand in a freely competitive market. Therefore the impact of a minimum wage law tends to be greater on young beginners— especially teenage workers— whose unemployment rates are especially relevant as tests of the economic principles which suggest that minimum wage laws create higher rates of unemployment.

With all the official statistics available, it might seem as if differences of opinion on this subject would have been resolved long ago. But, over the years, vast amounts of ingenuity have been deployed, seeking to evade the obvious, as regards the effects of minimum wage laws. Rather than elaborate and examine those arguments here, which have been elaborated and examined elsewhere,[23] a few plain facts may be sufficient.

In 1948, the unemployment rate in the United States for black 16-year-old males and black 17-year-old males was 9.4 percent. For their white counterparts, the unemployment rate was 10.2 percent. For black 18-year-old males and black 19-year-old males, their unemployment rate was 10.5 percent, and for their white counterparts the unemployment rate was 9.4 percent.[24] In short, there were no significant racial differences in unemployment rates among teenage males in 1948.

While an unemployment rate of around 10 percent for young, inexperienced workers is higher than the usual unemployment rate among workers in the population at large, it was lower than usual for teenagers. More important, for examining the effects of minimum wage laws on unemployment, these unemployment rates for teenage males were only a *fraction* of what unemployment rates for teenage males of both races would be from the 1970s onward, extending on into the early twenty-first century.[25]

Was there no minimum wage law in 1948? Was there no racism? Actually, there were both. But the federal minimum wage law— the Fair Labor Standards Act of 1938— was a decade old in 1948, and the intervening years had such high rates of inflation that the minimum wage specified in 1938 was well below what even an unskilled teenage male beginner (such as myself in 1948) was paid in the devalued dollars of 1948. For all practical purposes, there was no *effective* minimum wage law. As Professor George J. Stigler, a leading economist of that era, said in 1946: "The minimum wage provisions of the Fair Labor Standards act of 1938 have been repealed by inflation."[26]

In 1950, however, there began a series of increases in the minimum wage rate over the years, in order to keep up with inflation. The 1950s were the last decade in the twentieth century in which black

16-year-old and 17-year-old males had annual unemployment rates below 10 percent in any years. In later decades of that century, the annual unemployment rate of black teenage males *never fell below 20 percent*. In some of those years, it ranged above 40 percent. Moreover, there was now usually a substantially higher unemployment rate among black teenage males than among white teenage males. In some years, the difference exceeded two-to-one.[27]

Anyone who lived through those early years knows that there was *more* racism then than today. As late as 1950, public schools in Washington were explicitly segregated by race, and the General Accounting Office and some other federal agencies also had racially segregated employees, though not officially.[28] Why then was there no significant difference in unemployment rates between black and white teenage males in 1948? A short, one-word answer is economics.

Nobel Prize-winning economist Milton Friedman denounced minimum wage laws as "one of the most, if not the most, antiblack laws on the statute books."[29] One of his students, Gary S. Becker, went on to win a Nobel Prize in economics for his landmark work that included an in-depth analysis of the economics of discrimination.[30] The basic argument can be readily understood, without the technical vocabulary of economists.

Racism is an attitude inside people's heads, and may cost racists nothing. But discrimination is an overt act, out in the real world, that can cost the discriminator either little or much, depending on economic circumstances.[31] In a free competitive market, with prices determined by supply and demand, discrimination can have serious costs to the discriminator.

Minimum wage laws reduce the cost of discrimination to the discriminator. A wage rate set by government— at a level higher than it would be set by supply and demand in a competitive market— causes reactions by both workers and employers, as with other sellers and buyers who are not inert chess pieces.

Higher wage rates attract more job applicants. But these higher costs of labor tend to reduce the amount of labor employers hire. The net result is a chronic surplus of job applicants for low-wage jobs affected by minimum wage laws. In these circumstances, employers who turn away qualified minority applicants can often readily replace them with other qualified people from the chronic surplus of job applicants. Discrimination under these circumstances may cost the employer nothing.

When there is no minimum wage law, or no *effective* minimum wage law, as in 1948, there is unlikely to be a chronic surplus of job applicants. Under these conditions, employers who turn away qualified minority applicants would have to either pay more to attract additional other qualified applicants to replace them, or else work existing employees overtime, at higher overtime rates of pay— costing the employer money in either case.

In these circumstances, it is not surprising that there was no significant difference in unemployment rates between black and white male teenagers in 1948, even though there was more racism then than in later years. Nor is it surprising that, after a series of minimum wage rate increases over the years, to offset inflation and make the minimum wage law effective again, a substantial racial gap in teenage male unemployment rates became common. So did much higher unemployment rates for teenage males of both races, than what their unemployment rates had been in 1948, when wage rates were largely determined by supply and demand.

In general, the cost of discrimination to the discriminator can vary considerably from one kind of economic activity to another— being higher for businesses in competitive markets, where the employer's own money is at risk, than among non-profit organizations, regulated public utilities and government agencies. History shows that these last three kinds of institutions have long been among the most discriminatory kinds of employers.[32]

It costs government discriminators nothing to discriminate, because the costs are paid by the taxpayers. Similarly for discriminators in non-profit institutions, where employers are likewise spending other people's money. The situation in government-regulated public utilities is somewhat more complicated, but the net result is that these public utilities' costs of discrimination can be passed on to their customers, who have no choice but to pay, when dealing with a government-regulated monopoly.[33]

Each of these three kinds of institutions has had a long history of especially discriminatory policies against minority workers, as compared to policies in institutions operating in competitive markets, with employers' own money being at risk.[34] Prior to World War II, for example, black professors were virtually non-existent in white, non-profit colleges and universities. But there were hundreds of black chemists employed in profit-based businesses in competitive industries during that same era.[35] Such patterns were not confined to the United States or to blacks.

The pattern of most discrimination where it costs the discriminators least, and least discrimination where it costs the discriminators most, is a pattern found in many countries. In Poland between the two World Wars, for example, Jews were 9.8 percent of the population in 1931,[36] and just over half of all private physicians in Poland were Jewish. But Jewish physicians were seldom hired by Poland's government hospitals.[37] Other people, spending their own money, and concerned about their own health, obviously acted differently, or so many Jewish physicians would not have been able to make a living.

During even the worst days of racially discriminatory laws in South Africa under officially declared white supremacy policies, there were some whole occupations set aside by law exclusively for whites. But, nevertheless, there were some competitive industries where a majority of the employees in those occupations were in fact black.[38] A government crackdown fined hundreds of companies in the construction industry alone for having more black employees than they were allowed to have under the apartheid laws, and in occupations where they were forbidden to hire any blacks.[39]

How the severity of racial discrimination in South Africa during that era varied with the kind of industry, and the degree of government control, was revealed in *South Africa's War Against Capitalism* by black American economist Walter E. Williams, who did his research in South Africa during the era of apartheid.

Neither social justice advocates nor anyone else can safely proceed on the assumption that the particular laws and policies they prefer will automatically have the results they expect, without taking into account how the people on whom these laws and policies are imposed will react. Both history and economics show that people are not just inert chess pieces, carrying out someone else's grand design.

CHESS PIECES AND INCOME STATISTICS

In controversies revolving around social justice issues, some of the most serious distortions of reality are based on statistics showing income distribution trends over time. The statistics may be perfectly accurate, but the distortions come from discussing people as if they were like inert chess pieces, and remained fixed in the same income brackets over time.

Trends Over Time

The *New York Times,* for example, has said that "the gap between rich and poor has widened in America."[40] This has long been a theme common in such other media outlets as the *Washington Post* and many television programs, as well as among politicians and academics.

As a *Washington Post* columnist put it: "The rich have seen far greater income gains than have the poor."[41] Another *Washington Post* columnist described "the wealthy" as "people who have made almost all the income gains in recent years."[42] President Barack Obama said, "The top 10 percent no longer takes in one-third of our income, it now takes half."[43] Professor Joseph E. Stiglitz of Columbia University declared that "The upper 1 percent of Americans are now taking in nearly a quarter of the nation's income every year."[44] According to Professor Stiglitz, "society's wealth distribution" has become "lopsided."[45] By contrast, the other "99 percent of Americans" are said to be together "in the same stagnating boat."[46]

If these were the same people in the same income brackets over the years, the conclusions reached would be valid. *But these are not the same people in the same brackets over the years.* According to the U.S. Department of the Treasury, using income data from its Internal Revenue Service: "More than 50 percent of taxpayers in the bottom quintile moved to a higher quintile within ten years."[47] Other empirical studies show a similar pattern.[48] One study indicated that more than half of all American adults are in the top 10 percent of income recipients at some point in their lives,[49] usually in their later years. Whether at high income levels or low income levels, most Americans do not stay fixed in the same income bracket, as if they were inert chess pieces.

Other empirical studies that followed the incomes of *specific individuals* over a span of years also showed a pattern directly the opposite of the pattern in widely cited studies which implicitly assume that the same people remain in the same income brackets over the years. But a built-in *assumption* of stagnation is not stagnation, when there is *turnover* of most individuals in these brackets from one decade to the next.

An early study at the University of Michigan followed specific individuals— working Americans— from 1975 to 1991. The pattern it found was that individuals who were initially in the bottom 20 percent in income in 1975 had their incomes rise over the years— not only at a higher rate than the incomes of individuals in the higher brackets, but also in a several times larger total amount.[50] By 1991, 29 percent of those who were in the lowest quintile in 1975 had risen all the way to the top quintile, and only 5 percent of those initially in the bottom quintile remained where they had all been in 1975. The rest were distributed in other quintiles in between.[51]

These are not fictional Horatio Alger stories about rare individuals rising from rags to riches. These are mundane realities about people usually having higher incomes in their thirties than they had in their twenties, and continuing to have increases in pay as they acquire more experience, skills and maturity.

Meanwhile, individuals who were initially in the *top* quintile in 1975 had the *smallest* increase in real income by 1991— smallest in both percentage terms and in absolute amounts. The amount by which the average income of people initially in the top quintile in 1975 rose was less than half that in any of the other quintiles.[52] The pattern of these results— radically different from conclusions in studies which implicitly assume that it is the same people in the same income brackets over the years— was repeated in the later study by the U.S. Treasury

Department, already cited. This later study, based on Internal Revenue Service data, followed specific individuals— those who filed income tax returns over the course of a decade, from 1996 through 2005.

Those individuals whose incomes were initially in the bottom quintile of this group had their incomes rise by 91 percent during that decade. That is, their incomes nearly doubled in a decade, which is hardly "stagnating," Professor Stiglitz to the contrary notwithstanding. Those individuals whose incomes were initially in the much-discussed "top 1 percent" saw their incomes actually *fall* by 26 percent during that same decade.[53] Again, we see the *opposite* of what has been said repeatedly, loudly and angrily by income distribution alarmists in politics, in the media and in academia.

A still later statistical study, in Canada— covering the years from 1990 to 2009— showed a very similar pattern. During those two decades, 87 percent of the people initially in the bottom quintile rose into a higher quintile. The incomes of those initially in the bottom quintile rose at both a higher rate and a larger absolute amount than the incomes of those who were initially in the top quintile.[54]

It might seem as if these three studies, so similar in their outcomes, could not be true if the other and more widely cited studies— from the U.S. Bureau of the Census and other sources— were also true. But the two sets of studies measured very different things.

The University of Michigan study, the Treasury Department study and the Canadian study were all studies that followed *the same individuals* over a span of years. The more widely cited studies, from the U.S. Bureau of the Census and other sources using an approach similar to that of the Bureau of the Census, have been fundamentally different in at least two ways.

Published data from the 2020 census or the Bureau of Labor Statistics, for example, are data on statistical categories containing *multiple* individuals each, such as families, households or "consumer units." But, just as different families contain different numbers of individuals, so do these other statistical categories. When these categories of income recipients are divided into income quintiles, these quintiles can contain equal numbers of such categories, but *not* equal numbers of people— nor even approximately equal numbers of people.

Different Numbers of People

According to the Bureau of Labor Statistics, there were 42,187,200 people in the bottom quintile of income recipients in 2019. That same year, the B.L.S. statistics showed that the top quintile contained 84,915,200 people— just barely more than twice as many people as the bottom quintile.[55] Comparisons of the incomes received by people in the top and bottom quintiles therefore have a built-in exaggeration of income disparities between individuals, since twice as many individuals would have twice as much income, even if every individual in both categories had the *same* income.

When single-parent families are more common among low-income people than among high-income people, it is hardly surprising that there are fewer people in the bottom quintile than in the top quintile. Not only are fewer people likely to *receive* less income, that is especially so when discussing how much money they *earn*— as distinguished from money received from such sources as welfare or unemployment compensation. Bureau of Labor Statistics data show that there were *5 times* as many people earning income in the top quintile as in the bottom quintile.[56]

How surprising— or unfair— is it when 5 times as many people who are earning incomes receive a larger total amount of income?

People who draw alarming inferences from Census and similar other data reason as if they are discussing what was happening to a given set of human beings, when in fact they are discussing the fate of "the top quintile," "the top ten percent," "the top 1 percent" or some other statistical category. These are categories containing *different numbers of individuals* in different quintiles, as well as *an ever-changing mix of individuals* in each of these quintiles from one decade to the next.

What are the implications of all this?

If, for example, there were a complete redistribution of income, so that every income recipient recorded in the 2020 census now received exactly the same income as other recipients in a subsequent year, that would mean a *zero* disparity in individual incomes. But, if the new income data were organized and displayed in the same separate categories as before, comparing the same sets of individuals who had previously been in the various quintiles in the 2020 census, the data would show those people who had formerly been in the top quintile would now appear to have just over *twice* the incomes of those people who had formerly been in the bottom quintile.

In other words, a *zero* income disparity in fact would now appear statistically as an income disparity larger than today's income disparity between women and men or between black and white Americans!

"Stagnating" Income Growth

There is also a long history of alarmist claims about supposedly "stagnating" income growth among Americans as a whole. For example, the average real income— that is, money income adjusted for inflation— of American households rose by only 6 percent over a period of more than a quarter of a century, from 1969 to 1996. But the average real income per person in the United States rose by 51 percent over that very same period.[57] How can both these statistics be true? Because the average number of people per household was *declining* during those years. The Bureau of the Census stated, as far back as 1966, that the average number of persons per household was declining.[58]

Income alarmists have their choice of statistics to use. A *New York Times* writer said: "The incomes of most American households have failed to gain ground on inflation since 1973."[59] A *Washington Post* writer said: "the incomes of most American households have remained stubbornly flat over the past three decades."[60] An official of a Washington think tank was quoted in the *Christian Science Monitor* as saying: "The economy is growing without raising average living standards."[61]

Sometimes such conclusions may arise from statistical naivete. But sometimes the inconsistency of the patterns in which data are cited might suggest bias. Long-time *New York Times* columnist Tom Wicker, for example, used per capita income statistics when he depicted success for the Lyndon Johnson administration's economic policies, but he used family income statistics when he depicted failure for the policies of Ronald Reagan and George H.W. Bush.[62]

There is no intrinsic reason why the income distribution of *individuals* cannot be presented and analyzed, especially when incomes are in fact usually paid to individuals, rather than to families, households or "consumer units." But income distribution alarmists seldom, *if ever,* cite income statistics that compare the same individuals over time. As we have seen, such statistics show radically different results than the conclusions of income distribution alarmists.

Turnover in Income Brackets

The turnover rate of individuals is especially high in the highest income brackets. What Professor Paul Krugman of the City University of New York has referred to as "the charmed circle of the 1 percent"[63] must have a somewhat fleeting charm, because most of the people in that circle in 1996 were no longer there in 2005.[64] Neither high-income people nor low-income people are like inert chess pieces.

The turnover rate is even more extreme among the "top 400" highest income recipients than among the "top 1 percent." The Internal Revenue Service's income tax data showed that, during the years from 1992 to 2014, there were 4,584 people in the so-called "top 400" income recipients. Of these, 3,262 were in that bracket just one year during those 23 years[65]— which is within one generation.

When incomes received by thousands of people over the years are presented statistically as if these were incomes received by hundreds of people, that is a tenfold exaggeration of income disparities. If, as sometimes claimed, "the rich" have "rigged the system," it seems strange that they would rig it so that 71 percent of them would not repeat their one year in that high income bracket during the 23 years covered by the Internal Revenue Service data.

The "Rich" and The "Poor"

The loose use of words in many discussions of income differences includes calling people in the top quintile of income recipients "rich" and those in the bottom quintile "poor." But, in the 2020 census data, the top quintile begins with a household income of $141,111.[66] That is a very nice income for an individual, and perhaps somewhat less

impressive for a couple making just under $75,000 a year each—
especially if these people have risen to that income level from more
modest income levels, over the years. But in neither case would such
people be considered "rich," or able to afford the lifestyle of genuinely
rich people with their own mansions, yachts or private planes.

The "poor" are often as misleadingly labeled as "the rich." In the
University of Michigan study, where 95 percent of the people initially
in the bottom quintile rose out of that quintile during the years covered,
that left just 5 percent behind during those years. Since 5 percent of
the 20 percent initially in the bottom quintile was just 1 percent of
the population sampled, only this 1 percent, who were in the bottom
quintile for the duration of that study, were therefore eligible to be
called "poor" during all those years. Contrary to Professor Stiglitz's
claim that the incomes of the 99 percent were "stagnating,"[67] it is the
incomes of this low-income 1 percent that was stagnating.

How poor are "the poor"? Compared to what? We may each
conceive of poverty in different ways, perhaps thinking of times and
places where poverty has meant hunger, cramped housing, ragged
clothing and other such afflictions. But poverty statistics are defined
by the government statisticians who collect and publish official data.
In these data, official "poverty" means whatever these statisticians say
it means. No more and no less.

By 2001, three-quarters of officially "poor" Americans had air-
conditioning, which only a third of all Americans had, just a generation
earlier, in 1971. Ninety-seven percent of people in official poverty in
2001 had color television, which less than half of all Americans had
in 1971. Seventy-three percent owned a microwave oven, which fewer
than 1 percent of Americans owned in 1971, and 98 percent of "the
poor" in 2001 had either a videocassette recorder or a DVD player,
which no one had in 1971.[68]

As for living in cramped quarters, the average American in
officially defined poverty had more space per person than the average
European— not the average European in poverty, but the average
European, period.[69]

None of this suggests that Americans living in poverty have no
problems. They often have more serious and even urgent problems

today as victims of crime and violence than in the past, when their material standard of living was not as high. But that is a major problem deserving long-overdue attention on its own, more so than a supposedly "stagnating" income problem.

The terms "rich" and "poor" are misleading in another and more fundamental sense. These terms apply to people's stock of wealth, not their flows of income. *Income* taxes do not tax wealth. Even taxing 100 percent of a billionaire's income would not stop that billionaire from remaining a billionaire, though it can stop others from becoming billionaires. Praise for some billionaires who publicly recommend higher *income* taxes may be somewhat excessive.

Implications for "Social Justice"

Attempts to verbally convert people currently in different income brackets into different social classes ignore turnover— especially in high-income brackets, where many people are transients with a one-year spike in income. Presumably it is flesh-and-blood human beings whose well-being we are concerned about, not disparities between statistical categories containing very different numbers of people and ever-changing mixes of people.

What is the significance of the fact that the share of income going to people in the top quintile has been growing? To the income redistributionists, it suggested that a given set of people was receiving— or "taking"— a larger share of society's total income. But, while this might have been a valid conclusion, if the people in the different income brackets had been continuous residents in those brackets, that was not the case when they were transients.

With more than half of all American adults reaching the top quintile (and even the top decile) in household income at some point in their lives,[70] the increased reward awaiting those who reach that level over the years has meant that there was now a higher pay-off for rising to the top. Such an outcome is consistent with the fact that the age of peak earnings has risen over time from the 35–44-year-olds to people 45–54 years old.[71] This in turn is consistent with the fact that technological development has made knowledge more valuable, relative to the physical vitality of youth. Since everyone ages, such an outcome does not automatically concentrate high incomes in particular social classes.

Statistics can be enormously valuable, for testing our beliefs against empirical evidence. But that requires careful attention to specific data, and to the words which accompany those data. As economist Alan Reynolds, a Senior Fellow at the Cato Institute, put it:

> Measuring the growth of incomes or the inequality of incomes is a little like Olympic figure skating— full of dangerous leaps and twirls and not nearly as easy as it looks. Yet the growth and inequality of incomes are topics that seem to inspire many people to form very strong opinions about very weak statistics.[72]

Chapter 4

KNOWLEDGE FALLACIES

For many social issues, the most important decision is *who makes the decision*. Both social justice advocates and their critics might agree that many consequential social decisions are best made by those who have the most relevant knowledge. But they have radically different assumptions as to who in fact has the most knowledge.

That is partly because they have radically different conceptions of what is defined as knowledge. Such differences of opinion as to what constitutes knowledge go back for centuries.[1]

CONFLICTING VISIONS OF KNOWLEDGE

Intellectuals' view of knowledge was satirized in a verse about nineteenth-century British scholar Benjamin Jowett, Master of Balliol College at Oxford University:

> My name is Benjamin Jowett.
> If it's knowledge, I know it.
> I am the master of this college.
> What I don't know isn't knowledge.

Many people do not regard all information as deserving to be called knowledge, or would not regard the possessors of some kinds of information as being as knowledgeable as possessors of some other kinds of information. A carpenter may know how to build a fence, and a physicist may know that $E=MC^2$. But, even if neither of them knows what the other knows, many people would consider the physicist more knowledgeable, whether because his knowledge required more study or an intellect capable of mastering more complex information.

Knowledge, however, does not exist in a simple hierarchy, with the kind of special knowledge taught in schools and colleges at the top, and more mundane knowledge at the bottom. Some knowledge— in either category— is more *consequential* than other knowledge, and that varies with specific circumstances and the kinds of decisions to be made, rather than varying with the complexity or elegance of the knowledge itself.

Consequential Knowledge

As an example of *consequential* knowledge— knowledge affecting decisions with meaningful consequences in people's lives— the officers in charge of the *Titanic* no doubt had much complex knowledge about the intricacies of ships and navigation on the seas. But the most consequential knowledge on a particular night was the mundane knowledge of the location of particular icebergs, because collision with an iceberg is what damaged and sank the *Titanic*.

Although mundane information and special kinds of information have both been called knowledge by some, they are not commensurable, but are very distinct. Moreover, the presumably higher knowledge does not automatically encompass the more mundane knowledge. Each can be consequential in particular circumstances. This means that the distribution of consequential knowledge in a given society can be very different, depending on what kind of knowledge is involved.

As another example of the role of mundane but consequential knowledge, when people migrate from one country to another, they seldom migrate randomly from all parts of the country they leave or settle randomly in all parts of the country they go to. Various kinds of mundane knowledge— information of a sort not taught in schools or colleges— can play major roles in the migration decisions of millions of human beings.

Two provinces in mid-nineteenth-century Spain, containing just 6 percent of the Spanish population, supplied 67 percent of the Spanish immigrants to Argentina. Moreover, when these immigrants arrived in Argentina, they lived clustered together in particular neighborhoods in

Buenos Aires.[2] Similarly, during the last quarter of the nineteenth century, nearly 90 percent of the Italian immigrants to Australia came from an area in Italy containing just 10 percent of that country's population.[3] Yet immigration to Australia remained substantial, over the years, from the same isolated places in Italy where most of these emigrants originated. By 1939, there were more people from some Italian villages living in Australia than remained behind in those same villages back in Italy.[4]

Immigrants in general tend to go to some very specific place in the destination country, where people from their home country— *people known to them personally*, and trusted— have already settled before. Such people can provide newcomers with very specific information about the particular places where these earlier immigrants live. This has been highly valuable knowledge about such basic things as where to get a job, find an affordable place to live, and numerous other mundane but consequential things in a new country with unknown people and many unknown things about the way of life in a society that is new to the immigrants.

Where this kind of knowledge happened to be available to people in particular places in Spain or Italy, people from those particular places had high rates of immigration, while many other places in these same countries that lacked such personal connections could have very few people emigrating. Contrary to implicit assumptions of random behavior by some social theorists, *people did not emigrate randomly from Spain in general to Argentina in general, or from Italy in general to Australia in general.*

It was much the same story with Germans immigrating to the United States. One study found some villages "practically transplanted from Germany to rural Missouri."[5] There was a similar pattern among German immigrants to urban places in America. Frankfort, Kentucky, was founded by people from Frankfurt, Germany, and Grand Island, Nebraska, was founded by Schleswig-Holsteiners.[6] Of all the people who emigrated from China to the United States in more than half a century prior to World War I, 60 percent came from Toishan, just one of 98 counties in one province in southern China.[7]

Such patterns have been the rule, not the exception, among other immigrants to other countries, including the Lebanese settling in

Colombia[8] and Jewish immigrants from Eastern Europe settling in particular parts of New York's Lower East Side slum neighborhood.[9]

These patterns of very specific ties to very specific places— based on very specific mundane but consequential knowledge of particular people in those places— extended into the social life of immigrants after their arrival and settlement. Most of the marriages that took place in nineteenth-century New York's Irish neighborhoods were marriages between people from the same county in Ireland.[10] It was much the same story in the Australian city of Griffith. In the years from 1920 to 1933, 90 percent of the Italian men who had emigrated from Venice, and gotten married in Australia, married Italian women who had also emigrated from Venice.[11] *People sort themselves out*, based on very specific information.

Such patterns have been so widely observed that they have been given a name— "chain migration"— for the chain of personal connections involved. This is *consequential* knowledge, valued for its practical applications, rather than because of its intellectual challenge or elegance. It is a highly specific kind of knowledge, about highly specific people and places. This kind of knowledge is unlikely to be known by surrogate decision-makers, such as economic central planners or policy experts, who may have far more of the kinds of knowledge taught in schools and colleges. But, no matter how much of this latter kind of knowledge may be regarded as *higher* knowledge, it does not necessarily encompass— much less supersede— what is regarded as lower knowledge.

How much knowledge there is in a given society, and how it is distributed, depends crucially on how knowledge is conceived and defined. When a social justice advocate like Professor John Rawls of Harvard referred to how "society" should "arrange" certain outcomes,[12] he was clearly referring to collective decisions of a kind that a government makes, using knowledge available to surrogate decision-makers, more so than the kind of knowledge known and used by individuals in the population at large, when making their own decisions about their own lives. As an old saying expressed it: "A fool can put on his coat better than a wise man can do it for him."[13]

Whatever the desirability of the goals sought by social justice advocates, the *feasibility* of achieving those goals through surrogate decision-makers depends on the distribution of relevant and consequential knowledge.

It also depends on the nature, purpose and reliability of the political process through which governments act. The history of many twentieth-century fervent crusades for idealistic goals is a painful record of how often the granting of great powers to governments, in pursuit of those goals, led instead to totalitarian dictatorships. The bitter theme of "the Revolution betrayed" goes back at least as far as the French Revolution in the eighteenth century.

At the opposite pole from the position attributed to Benjamin Jowett, twentieth-century Nobel Prize-winning economist F.A. Hayek's conception of knowledge would encompass both the carpenter's information and the physicist's information— and extend far beyond both. This put him in direct opposition to various systems of surrogate decision-making in the twentieth century, including the social justice vision.

To Hayek, consequential knowledge included not only articulated information, but also *unarticulated* information, embodied in behavioral responses to known realities. Examples might include something as simple— and consequential— as putting warm clothing on children before taking them out in cold weather, or moving your car over to the side of a road, when you hear the siren of an emergency vehicle wanting to pass. As Hayek put it:

> Not all knowledge in this sense is part of our intellect, nor is our intellect the whole of our knowledge. Our habits and skills, our emotional attitudes, our tools, and our institutions— all are in this sense adaptations to past experience which have grown up by selective elimination of less suitable conduct. They are as much an indispensable foundation of successful action as is our conscious knowledge.[14]

This sweeping definition of knowledge radically changes how the distribution of knowledge is seen. Consequential knowledge, as conceived by Hayek, is far more widely spread among the population at large— often in individually unimpressive fragments that will have to be coordinated by people's individual interactions with each other, in order to achieve mutual accommodations, as in economic market transactions, for example.

Another economist, Leonard Read, pointed out that no individual possesses all the knowledge required to produce all the components of a simple, inexpensive lead pencil. Market transactions bring together— from different parts of the world— the graphite used for writing, the rubber for the eraser, the wood in which these things are embedded and the metal band that holds the eraser on.

No given individual is likely to know how to produce all these very different things, often originating in very different places, and using very different technologies. Inexpensive pencils are produced through chains of information and cooperation, in market transactions based on condensed but consequential knowledge, conveyed in the form of prices, which in turn are based on competition between a variety of producers of each component. A manufacturer brings all these components of the pencil together, at a cost that consumers are willing to pay.

The implications of all this for the social justice vision depend not only on the desirability of the goals of that vision, but also on the feasibility of using particular kinds of institutions through which such goals might be pursued. It is not enough to say, as Professor Rawls said, that "society" should "arrange" to produce certain outcomes[15]— *somehow*. The choices of institutional mechanisms matter, not only from the standpoint of economic efficiency, but even more so for the sake of preserving the freedom of millions of people to make their own decisions about their own lives as they see fit, rather than have surrogate decision-makers preempt their decisions, in the name of noble-sounding words, such as "social justice."

The convenient vagueness of referring to "society" as the decision-maker to "arrange" outcomes— as in Rawls' vision of social justice[16]— was preceded by Progressive-era philosopher John Dewey's similarly vague references to "social control" to replace "chaotic" and narrowly "individualistic" decisions in market economies.[17] Before that, back in the eighteenth century, there was Rousseau's vague "general will" for making decisions for the sake of "the common good."[18]

Very different conceptions of decision-making processes reflect very different beliefs about the distribution of consequential knowledge. It is understandable that people with very different conceptions of knowledge and its distribution reach very different conclusions as to which kinds of institutions produce better or worse outcomes for human beings.

Opposite Visions

Although F.A. Hayek was a landmark figure in the development of an understanding of the crucial role of the distribution of knowledge in determining which kinds of policies and institutions were likely to produce what kinds of results, there were others before him whose analyses had similar implications, and others after him— notably Milton Friedman— who applied Hayek's analysis in their own work.

An opposite vision of knowledge and its distribution has likewise had a very long pedigree behind its opposite conclusions— namely, that consequential knowledge is concentrated in intellectually more advanced people. The question of what constitutes knowledge was among the things addressed in a two-volume 1793 treatise titled *Enquiry Concerning Political Justice* by William Godwin.[19]

Godwin's conception of knowledge was very much like that prevalent in today's writings on social justice. Indeed, the word "political" in the title of his book was used in a sense common at that time, referring to the polity or governmental structure of a society. The word was used in a similar sense at that time in the expression "political economy"— meaning what we call "economics" today— the economic analysis of a society or polity, as distinguished from economic analysis of decisions in a home, business or other individual institution within a society or polity.

To Godwin, explicitly articulated reason was the source of knowledge and understanding. In this way, "just views of society" in the minds of "the liberally educated and reflecting members" of society will enable them to be "to the people guides and instructors."[20] Here the assumption of superior knowledge and understanding did not lead to casting an intellectual elite in the role of surrogate decision-makers as part of a government, but as influencers of the public, who in turn were expected to influence the government.

A similar role for the intellectual elite appeared later in the nineteenth-century writings of John Stuart Mill. Although Mill saw the population at large as having more knowledge than the government,[21] he also saw the population as needing the guidance of elite intellectuals. As he said in *On Liberty*, democracy can rise above mediocrity, only where "the sovereign Many have let themselves be guided (which in their best times they always have done) by the counsels and influence of a more highly gifted and instructed One or Few."[22]

Mill depicted these intellectual elites— "the best and wisest,"[23] the "thinking minds,"[24] "the most cultivated intellects in the country,"[25] "those who have been in advance of society in thought and feeling"[26]— as "the salt of the earth; without them, human life would become a stagnant pool."[27] He called on the universities to "send forth into society a succession of minds, not the creatures of their age, but capable of being its improvers and regenerators."[28]

Ironically, this presumed indispensability of intellectuals for human progress was asserted at a time and in a place— nineteenth-century Britain— where an industrial revolution was taking place in Mill's own lifetime that would change whole patterns of life in many nations around the world. Moreover, this industrial revolution was led by men with practical experience in industry, rather than intellectual or scientific education. Among Americans as well, even revolutionary industrial giants like Thomas Edison and Henry Ford had very little formal schooling,[29] and the first airplane to lift off the ground with a human being on board was invented by two bicycle mechanics— the Wright brothers— who never finished high school.[30]

Nevertheless, John Stuart Mill's vision of the indispensable role of intellectuals in human progress has been one shared by many intellectuals over the centuries. These have included intellectuals leading crusades for more economic equality, based ironically on assumptions of their own superiority. Rousseau said in the eighteenth century that he considered it "the best and most natural arrangement for the wisest to govern the multitude."[31] Variations on this theme have marked such movements against economic inequality as Marxism, Fabian socialism, Progressivism and social justice activism.

Rousseau, despite his emphasis on society being guided by "the general will," left the interpretation of that will to elites. He likened the masses of the people to "a stupid, pusillanimous invalid."[32] Others on the eighteenth-century left, such as William Godwin and the Marquis de Condorcet, expressed similar contempt for the masses.[33] In the nineteenth century, Karl Marx said, "The working class is revolutionary or it is nothing."[34] In other words, millions of fellow human beings mattered only if they carried out the Marxian vision.

Fabian socialist pioneer George Bernard Shaw regarded the working class as being among the "detestable" people who "have no right to live." He added: "I should despair if I did not know that they will all die presently, and that there is no need on earth why they should be replaced by people like themselves."[35]

In our own times, prominent legal scholar Professor Ronald Dworkin of Oxford University declared that "a more equal society is a better society even if its citizens prefer inequality."[36] French feminist pioneer Simone de Beauvoir likewise said, "No woman should be authorized to stay at home to raise her children. Society should be totally different. Women should not have that choice, precisely because if there is such a choice, too many women will make that one."[37] In a similar vein, consumer activist Ralph Nader said that "the consumer must be protected at times from his own indiscretion and vanity."[38]

We have already seen how similar attitudes led genetic determinists in the early twentieth century to casually advocate imprisoning people who had committed no crime, and denying them a normal life, on the basis of unsubstantiated beliefs that were then in vogue in intellectual circles.

Given the conception of knowledge prevalent among many elite intellectuals, and the distribution of such knowledge implied by that conception, it is hardly surprising that they reach the kinds of conclusions that they do. Indeed, to make the opposite assumption— that one's own great achievements and competence are confined to a narrow band, out of the vast spectrum of human concerns— could be a major impediment to promoting social crusades that preempt the decisions of others, who are supposedly to be the beneficiaries of such crusades as the quest for social justice.

F.A. Hayek regarded the assumptions of crusading intellectuals as *The Fatal Conceit*— the title of his book on the subject. Although he was a landmark figure in opposition to the presumed superiority of intellectuals as guides or surrogate decision-makers for other people, he was not alone in his opposition to the idea of a presumed concentration of consequential knowledge in intellectual elites.

Professor Milton Friedman, another Nobel Prize economist, noted how that honor can lead to assumptions of omnicompetence, by both the public and the recipient:

> It is a tribute to the worldwide repute of the Nobel awards that the announcement of an award converts its recipient into an instant expert on all and sundry... Needless to say the attention is flattering, but also corrupting.[39]

Yet another Nobel laureate, Professor George J. Stigler, likewise observed: "A full collection of public statements signed by laureates whose work gave them not even professional acquaintance with the problem addressed by the statement would be a very large and somewhat depressing collection."[40] He referred to "Nobel laureates who issue stern ultimata to the public on almost a monthly basis, and sometimes on no other basis."[41]

Such presumptions of omnicompetence have by no means been confined to Nobel laureates. Professor Friedman found such beliefs common among prominent individuals and institutions promoting social crusades currently in vogue:

> I talked to and argued with groups from academia, from the media, from the financial community, from the foundation world, from you name it. I was appalled at what I found. There was an unbelievable degree of intellectual homogeneity, of acceptance of a standard set of views complete with cliché answers to every objection, of smug self-satisfaction at belonging to an in-group.[42]

It is unusual for what critics say about some people to be so similar to what those people say about themselves— in this case, how intellectual elites feel so superior to other people. This pattern goes back at least as far as the eighteenth century, and is consistent with what John Maynard Keynes said in the twentieth century about the intellectual circle to which he had belonged:

> We entirely repudiated a personal liability on us to obey general rules. We claimed the right to judge every individual case on its merits, and the wisdom, experience and self-control to do so successfully... Before heaven we claimed to be our own judge in our own case.[43]

Although, in his later years, Keynes recognized some of the problems with that approach, he nevertheless said: "Yet so far as I am concerned, it is too late to change."[44] A biographer of Keynes, a fellow economist who was his contemporary, pointed out another aspect of Keynes' character that has long been characteristic of some other intellectual elites:

> He held forth on a great range of topics, on some of which he was thoroughly expert, but on others of which he may have derived his views from the few pages of a book at which he had happened to glance. The air of authority was the same in both cases.[45]

Differences in assumptions about the distribution of consequential knowledge are more than incidental social curiosities. People seeking similar goals can reach radically different conclusions about the way to achieve those goals, when they have radically different beliefs about the nature and distribution of the consequential knowledge required. In some cases, the goals themselves can seem possible or impossible, depending on what kind of knowledge distribution would be required to reach those goals.

FACTS AND MYTHS

Policies based on the social justice vision tend to assume not only a concentration of consequential knowledge in intellectual elites, but also a concentration of the causes of socioeconomic disparities in such other people as heads of business, educational and other institutions. Accordingly, the social justice agenda tends to focus its attention on correcting institutional and societal defects by having government empower surrogate decision-makers to rescue victims of various forms of mistreatment by taking many decisions out of other people's hands. This has included taking some decisions out of the hands of the supposed victims themselves, and transferring those decisions to elite surrogates, whose supposedly greater knowledge could better protect their interests.

These preemptions of other people's decisions for their own good has ranged from decisions about employment and personal finance to decisions about housing and the values to be taught to their children.

Advocacy of such preemptions was a prominent feature of the Progressive era in early twentieth-century America, and has continued on into the present.

Employment Issues

One of the prominent early Progressives to call for elite preemptions of other people's decisions was Walter E. Weyl, who graduated from college at age 19, went on to earn a Ph.D., and had a career as an academic and a journalist. He was clearly one of the intellectual elites, and he devoted his talents to crusading for a "socialized democracy," in which employees would be protected from the "great interstate corporations,"[46] among other hazards and restrictions. For example:

> A law forbidding a woman to work in the textile mills at night is a law increasing rather than restricting *her* liberty, simply because it takes from the employer *his* former right to compel her through

sheer economic pressure to work at night when she would prefer to work by day.[47]

Clearly, Walter E. Weyl saw the employer as taking away this woman's liberty and people like himself as wanting to restore it to her— even though it was the employer who offered her an option and surrogates like Weyl who wanted to take away her option. For intellectual elites who see society's consequential knowledge concentrated in people like themselves, this might make sense. But people who see consequential knowledge widely diffused among the population at large could reach the opposite conclusion— already mentioned— that "A fool can put on his coat better than a wise man can do it for him." Or her.

Minimum wage laws are another example of intellectual elites and social justice advocates acting as surrogate decision-makers, preempting the decisions of both employers and employees. As noted in Chapter 3, the unemployment rate among black 16-year-old and 17-year-old males was under 10 percent in 1948, when inflation had rendered the minimum wage law ineffective. But, after a series of minimum wage increases, beginning in 1950, restored that law's effectiveness, the unemployment rate of black males in this age bracket rose, and *never fell below 20 percent* for more than three consecutive decades, in the years from 1958 to 1994.[48]

In some of those years, their unemployment rate was over *40* percent. Moreover, during those years, the virtually identical unemployment rates for black and white teenage males that existed when the minimum wage law was ineffective in 1948, now had a racial gap. Black teenage male unemployment rates were now often twice as high as the unemployment rate for white teenage males.[49] In 2009— ironically, the first year of the Obama administration— the annual unemployment rate of black teenage males as a whole was 52 percent.[50]

In other words, half of all black teenage males looking for jobs could not find any, because surrogate decision-makers made it illegal for them to take jobs at wages that employers were willing to pay, but which third-party surrogates disliked. Preempting their options left black teenage males the choice of doing without pay in legal occupations or making money from illegal activities, such as selling drugs— an activity with dangers from both the law and rival gangs. But even if unemployed black teenage males just hung around idle on the streets, no community of any race is made better off with many adolescent males hanging around with nothing useful to do.

None of these facts has made the slightest impression on many people advocating higher minimum wage rates. This is another example of situations in which "friends" and "defenders" of the less fortunate are oblivious to the harm they are doing. *New York Times* columnist Nicholas Kristof, for example, depicted people who oppose minimum wage laws as people with "hostility" to "raising the minimum wage to keep up with inflation"because of their "mean-spiritedness"or "at best, a lack of empathy toward those struggling."[51]

There is no need to attribute malign intentions to Nicholas Kristof. Fact-free moralizing is a common pattern among social justice advocates. But the fundamental problem is an institutional problem, when laws allow third-party surrogates to preempt other people's decisions and *pay no price for being wrong*, no matter how high the price paid by others, whom they are supposedly helping.

Anyone seriously interested in facts about the effects of minimum wage laws on employment can find such facts in innumerable examples from countries around the world, and in different periods of history.[52] Most modern, industrial countries have minimum wage laws, but some do not, so their unemployment levels can be compared to the unemployment levels in other countries.

It was news in 2003 when *The Economist* magazine reported that Switzerland's unemployment rate "neared a five-year high of 3.9% in February."[53] Switzerland had no minimum wage law. The city-state of Singapore has also been without a minimum wage law, and its unemployment rate has been as low as 2.1 percent in 2013.[54] Back in 1991, when Hong Kong was still a British colony, it too had no minimum wage law, and its unemployment rate was under 2 percent.[55] The last American administration without a national minimum wage law was the Coolidge administration in the 1920s. In President Coolidge's last four years in office, the annual unemployment rate ranged from a high of 4.2 percent to a low of 1.8 percent.[56]

While some social justice advocates may think of minimum wage laws as a way to help low-income people, many special-interest groups in countries around the world— perhaps more experienced and informed about their own economic interests— have deliberately advocated minimum wage laws for the express purpose of pricing some low-income people out of the labor market. At one time, the groups targeted for exclusion included Japanese immigrant workers in Canada[57] and African workers in South Africa under apartheid,[58] among others.[59]

Payday Loans

Similar presumptions have led to many local social justice crusades to outlaw so-called "payday loans" in low-income neighborhoods. These are usually short-term loans of small amounts of money, charging something like $15 per hundred dollars lent for perhaps a few weeks.[60] Low-income people, facing some unexpected financial emergency, often turn to such loans because banks are unlikely to lend to them, and the money they need to deal with some emergency must be paid before their next check is due— whether that is a paycheck from some job, or a check from welfare or some other source.

Perhaps an old car has broken down, and needs immediate repairs, if that is the only way someone can get to work from where they live. Or a family member might have suddenly gotten sick, and needs some expensive medicine right away. In any event, the borrowers need money they don't have, and they need it *right now*. Paying $15 to borrow $100 until the end of the month may be one of the very few options available. But that could work out mathematically to an annual interest rate of several hundred percent— and social justice advocates consider that "exploitation." Accordingly, payday loans have been denounced from the editorial pages of the *New York Times*[61] to many other venues for social justice activism.[62]

By the same kind of reasoning as that denouncing payday loan interest rates as being several hundred percent on an annual basis, renting a hotel room for $100 a night is paying $36,500 rent annually, which seems exorbitant for renting a room. But of course most people are very unlikely to rent a hotel room for a year at that price. Nor is there any guarantee to the hotel management that every room in a hotel will be rented every night, even though hotel employees have to be paid every payday, regardless of how many rooms are rented or not rented.

Nevertheless, based on reasoning about annual interest rates, some states have imposed interest rate caps, which have often been enough to shut down most payday loan businesses. Among the other flaws in the social justice crusaders' reasoning is that the $15 is not all interest, as economists define interest. That sum also covers the cost of processing the loan and covers the inevitable risks of losses from any kind of lending, as well as covering such common business expenses as employees' salaries, rent, etc., that other businesses have.

Such costs are a higher percentage of all costs when a small amount of money is borrowed. It does not cost a bank a hundred times as much to process a loan of $10,000 as it costs a payday loan business to process a loan of $100.

In short, the real interest rate— net of other costs— is unlikely to be anything resembling the alarming interest rate numbers that are thrown around recklessly, in order to justify preempting the decisions of low-income people faced with a financial emergency. But, nevertheless, intellectual elites and social justice crusaders can go away feeling good about themselves, after depriving poor people of one of their very few options for dealing with a financial emergency.

To someone directly involved, it may be worth much more than $15 to avoid losing a day's pay or to spare a sick family member needless suffering. But it may never occur to crusading intellectual elites that ordinary people may have far more consequential knowledge about their own circumstances than distant surrogates have.

As for "exploitation," it is not always easy to know what some people mean specifically when they use that word, other than as an expression of their disapproval. But if we take "exploitation" in this context to mean that people who own payday loan businesses receive a higher rate of return on their business investment than is necessary to compensate them for being in this particular business, then the complete shutdown of many payday loan businesses, in the wake of legislation reducing their "interest" charges, suggests the opposite. Why would anyone completely give up a business that still earns them as much of a return on their investment as other businesses receive?

In the particular cases where legislated limits on what is called "interest" force payday loan businesses to go out of business, social justice reformers may go away feeling good about having ended "exploitation" of the poor, when they have in fact simply denied the poor one of their very few options in an emergency, by preventing the businesses supplying that option from earning a rate of return common in other businesses.

Housing Decisions

Even such basic individual decisions as where to live— in what kind of housing and in what kind of neighborhood— have been preempted by surrogate decision-makers.

For more than a century, social reformers have used the power of government to force low-income people to abandon the homes in which they have chosen to live, and move to places the reformers consider better. These policies have gone by a variety of names, such as "slum clearance," "urban renewal" or whatever other names happened to be in vogue politically at various times.

Some of the housing that the poorest people lived in, especially back in the early twentieth century, was truly awful. A survey in 1908 showed that about half of the families who lived on New York's Lower East Side had three or four people sleeping per room, and nearly 25 percent of these families had five or more people sleeping per room.[63] Individual home bathtubs were very rare in such places at that time. An indoor faucet or toilet, to be shared by many tenants, was a recent improvement, and they were by no means universal. There were still thousands of outdoor toilets in the backyards, which could be something of a challenge in the winter.

Surrogate decision-makers did not merely advise the tenants to leave, nor did the government provide places to which they could move. Instead, government officials ordered the slums torn down, and used the police to evict tenants who did not want to leave. During these and later times, surrogate decision-makers simply assumed that their own knowledge and understanding were superior to that of the low-income people they had forced out of the tenements. Later, after better housing was built as replacements, the surrogates could feel vindicated.

Even if both the housing that the evicted tenants moved into immediately and the new housing that was built to replace the slums were better, the slum tenants already had the former option before they were evicted— and their choice, when they had one, was to stay where they were, in order to save some much-needed money, rather than pay higher rent. Often the better housing that was built as replacements was also more expensive.

Among the poorest of the European immigrants at that time were Eastern European Jews. Their men often began working as peddlers on the streets, while the women and children worked at home— for long hours at low piecework pay, on consignments of clothing production in the slum apartments where they lived. They were often trying to save up enough money to be able to eventually open up some small shop or grocery store, in hopes of being able to earn a better living that way, or at least not having their men be peddlers working outdoors on the streets in all kinds of weather.

Many of these Jewish immigrants had family members back in Eastern Europe, where they were being attacked by anti-Semitic mobs. The money being saved was also used to pay the fares of those family members who desperately needed to escape. During these years, most of the Jewish immigrants from Eastern Europe who came to America had their fares paid by family members already living in America,[64] even though many Jews at that time were still poor and living in slums.

Other immigrant groups, living in slums in nineteenth-century and early twentieth-century America, had similarly urgent situations to deal with. Italian immigrants, who were overwhelmingly men, often had families back in the poorer southern regions of Italy, to whom they sent money they earned in the United States. These immigrants often slept many men to a room, in order to save money. Observers who noticed that they seemed to be physically smaller than other men— something not said of Italian men in America in later generations— may not have known that these men skimped even on food, in order to save up money with which to either return to Italy in a few years to rejoin their families, or to send money to their families to come join them in America.

In an earlier generation, Irish immigrants lived in some of the worst slums in America— usually in families, but also with other family members still remaining in Ireland, where a crop failure created a devastating famine that struck in the 1840s. Like the Jewish immigrants from Eastern Europe in later years, the Irish living in America sent money back to their family members in Ireland, so that they could immigrate to America, with their fares prepaid.[65]

These and other urgent reasons for needing to save money were part of the consequential knowledge keenly felt by family members living in the slums, but less likely to be known by surrogate decision-makers with great confidence in their own supposedly superior knowledge and understanding. Early Progressive-era writer Walter E. Weyl said that "a tenement house law increases the liberty of tenement dwellers."[66] The resistance of slum dwellers who had to be forced out by police suggests that they saw things differently.

Children

An even deeper penetration into the lives of other people has been preempting parents' role in raising their own children.

The decision as to when and how parents want their children to be informed and advised about sex was simply preempted by surrogates who introduced "sex education" into the public schools in the 1960s. Like so many other social crusades by intellectual elites, the "sex education" agenda was presented politically as an urgent response to an existing "crisis." In this case, the problems to be solved were said to include unwanted pregnancies among teenage girls and venereal diseases among both sexes.

A Planned Parenthood representative, for example, testified before a Congressional subcommittee on the need for such programs "to assist our young people in reducing the incidence of out-of-wedlock births and early marriage necessitated by pregnancy."[67] Similar views, as regards both venereal diseases and unwanted pregnancies were echoed in many elite intellectual circles, and questioners or critics were depicted as ignorant or worse.[68]

What were the actual facts, as of the time of this "crisis," supposedly in urgent need of a "solution" by preempting the role of parents? *Venereal diseases had been declining for years.* The rate of infection for gonorrhea declined every year from 1950 through 1958, and the rate of syphilis infection was, by 1960, less than half of what it had been in 1950.[69] The pregnancy rate among teenage females had declined for more than a decade.[70]

As for the facts about what happened *after* "sex education" was widely introduced into public schools, the rate of teenage gonorrhea tripled between 1956 and 1975.[71] The rate of infection for syphilis continued to decline, but its *rate* of decline from 1961 on was nowhere near as steep as its sharp rate of decline in earlier years.[72]

During the 1970s, the pregnancy rate among females from 15 years old to 19 years old rose from approximately 68 per thousand in 1970 to approximately 96 per thousand by 1980.[73] Data for *birth* rates per thousand females in this same age group differ numerically— because of abortions and miscarriages— but the *pattern* over the years was similar.

Beginning in the years before sex education was introduced into the public schools on a large scale in the 1960s, the birth rate among unmarried females, aged 15 to 19, was 12.6 per thousand in 1950, 15.3 in 1960, 22.4 in 1970 and 27.6 in 1980. At the end of the century in 1999, it was 40.4 per thousand.[74] As a percentage of all births to females in the same age bracket— both married and unmarried— the births to unmarried females in this age bracket were 13.4 percent of all the births to females of these ages in 1950, 14.8 in 1960, 29.5 in 1970, and 47.6 in 1980. As of the year 2000, more than three quarters of all the births to females in this age bracket— 78.7 percent— were to unmarried females.[75]

The reason is not hard to find: The percentage of unmarried teenage females who had engaged in sex was higher at every age from 15 through 19 by 1976 than it was just five years earlier.[76] Nor is it hard to understand why, when the specifics of what was called "sex education" included such things as this:

> A popular sex instructional program for junior high school students, aged 13 and 14, shows film strips of four naked couples, two

homosexual and two heterosexual, performing a variety of sexually explicit acts, and teachers are warned with a cautionary note from the sex educators not to show the materials to parents or friends: "Many of the materials of this program shown to people outside the context of the program itself can evoke misunderstanding and difficulties."[77]

When some parents in Connecticut learned of the specifics of such "sex education" programs and protested, they were denounced as "fundamentalists" and "right-wing extremists." It so happens that their religion is known, even if their political views are not. They were affluent Episcopalians.[78] But here, as with many other issues involving the social crusades of intellectual elites, arguments against their positions are too often answered by *ad hominem* denunciations, rather than by counter-arguments with facts. Among the comments from "experts" was that "sex and sexuality have become far too complex and technical to leave to the typical parent, who is either uninformed or too bashful to share useful sexual information with his child."[79]

Across a broad spectrum of issues, people who see themselves as possessors of superior consequential knowledge, lacking in other people, see no problem in preempting other people's decisions. Nor are consequences that are the opposite of what was predicted necessarily chastening. Many advocates of "sex education" in public schools used these dire consequences as showing an even more urgent need for additional "sex education."[80]

However, as in the case of the early Progressive-era genetic determinists, there was one prominent supporter of "sex education" in the public schools who frankly faced the facts. This was Sargent Shriver, former head of the Office of Economic Opportunity, which had led the early charge for "sex education" in public schools. He said in testimony before a Congressional committee in 1978:

Just as venereal disease has skyrocketed 350% in the last 15 years when we have had more clinics, more pills, and more sex education than ever in history, teen-age pregnancy has risen.[81]

As with Carl Brigham's recanting of his conclusions on genetic determinism in an earlier generation, it is hard to find others prepared to be equally frank.

PATTERNS AND CONSEQUENCES

In politics— whether electoral politics or ideological politics— the word "crisis" often means whatever situation someone wants to change. Far from automatically indicating some dire condition threatening the public, it often means simply a golden opportunity for surrogates to use the taxpayers' money and the government's power to advance the surrogates' interests, whether these interests are political, ideological or financial.

Intellectual elites crusading for their ideological goals have, for centuries, seen children as a special target for their messages. As far back as the eighteenth century, William Godwin said that children— *other people's children*— "are a sort of raw material put into our hands."[82] Their minds "are like a sheet of white paper."[83] This vision of teaching other people's children as a golden opportunity for intellectuals to shape society, by controlling what is inscribed on these young and presumably blank minds, has remained a key feature of social crusades to remake the world to fit the preconceptions of intellectual elites, who see themselves as key possessors of consequential knowledge.

This same conception of the educational role of crusading intellectual elites was a central feature of the Progressive era, in both the early twentieth century and the later twentieth century, continuing on into our own times. Before Progressive-era icon Woodrow Wilson became President of the United States, he was president of Princeton University. He saw his role as an educator to be "to make the young gentlemen of the rising generation as unlike their fathers as possible."[84] There was no suggestion of who gave him such a mandate— or even whether parents would tolerate, much less pay for, such a usurpation of their role, if they knew about it.

Another major figure of the early Progressive era, Professor John Dewey of Columbia University, likewise saw schools as places to help "eliminate obvious social evils" through the schools' "development of children and youth but also of the future society of which they will be the constituents."[85] Schools "train the State of to-morrow," according to Dewey, and could be instrumental in "overcoming the present defects of our system."[86] In short, "it is the business of the school environment to eliminate, so far as possible, the unworthy features of the existing environment," and be "weeding out" undesirable "dead wood from the past."[87] John Dewey has long been recognized as a major and lasting influence on the role of American public schools. Dewey's many writings on education seldom focused on such mundane concerns as how to get students to better understand mathematics, science or language. He clearly sought a more expansive role for educators as promoters of a Progressive vision of society— and doing so behind the backs of parents.

When Dewey created the Laboratory School at the University of Chicago, its goals were ideological— reflecting Dewey's own passionate feelings about political issues of the time— and especially a sense of need to change the economic and other institutions of American society.[88]

Ironically, many intellectual elites— then and now— seem to regard themselves as promoting a more *democratic* society, when they preempt other people's decisions. Their conception of democracy seems to be equalization of outcomes, by intellectual elites. This would confer benefits on the less fortunate, at the expense of those whom these surrogates consider less deserving. That is very different from democracy as a political system, based on free choices by members of the voting public, to determine what laws and policies they want to be governed by— and which individuals they want to put in charge of the government, to administer those laws and policies.

No prominent American more openly declared his rejection of democracy as political control by the voting public than President Woodrow Wilson. He rejected "popular sovereignty" as a basis for government, because he saw it as an obstacle impeding what he called "executive expertness."[89] Clearly, he saw consequential knowledge concentrated in elite "experts." He saw "the many, the people" as "selfish, ignorant, timid, stubborn, or foolish."[90] He deplored what he called "that besetting error of ours, the error of trying to do too much by vote."[91] He favored government by surrogate decision-makers, armed with superior knowledge and understanding— "executive expertness"— and unhindered by the voting public.

Woodrow Wilson's response to objections that this would deprive the people at large of the freedom to live their own lives as they saw fit, was to redefine the word "freedom." He used the phrase "the new freedom"[92] when running for President in 1912, and published a book with that title.[93] By simply depicting government-provided benefits— dispensed by surrogate decision-makers— as an *additional* freedom for the recipients, President Wilson made the issue of people's loss of freedom disappear, as if by verbal sleight of hand.

Whether the supposed beneficiaries of these policies would consider a trade-off of personal freedom for government benefits worthwhile was a question kept off the agenda by this redefinition of the word "freedom." Woodrow Wilson's book was subtitled "A Call for the Emancipation of the Generous Energies of a People" and was dedicated, "with all my heart," to people who would go into "unselfish public service."[94] Rhetorically, at least, people were being emancipated, rather than losing freedom.

Similar themes would be echoed again and again, over the years, by others, on into the twenty-first century. During the vast expansion of the American welfare state by the Lyndon Johnson administration in the 1960s, for example, a Cabinet member in that administration used the redefinition of freedom as increases of the kind of things that governments could provide, rather than as personal autonomy in one's own decisions and behavior:

> Only when he can support himself and his family, choose his job and make a living wage can an individual and his family exercise real freedom. Otherwise he is a servant to survival without the means to do what he wants to do.[95]

Some years later, a book by two Yale professors— *Politics, Economics, and Welfare*— likewise defined freedom in terms of things received, rather than autonomy preserved. As they expressed it, "we shall try to unravel some of the complexities in the theory and practice of freedom."[96] Their conception of freedom was "the absence of obstacles to the realisation of desires."[97] The "complexities" of this Wilsonian definition of freedom are certainly understandable, since evading the obvious can become very complex. When Spartacus led an uprising of slaves, back in the days of the Roman Empire, he was not doing it to get welfare state benefits.

The more sophisticated or "complex" redefinition of freedom has continued on into the twenty-first century. The author of a book titled *The Great Escape: Health, Wealth, and the Origins of Inequality* said: "In this book, when I speak of freedom, it is the freedom to live a good life and to do the things that make life worth living. The absence of freedom is poverty, deprivation, and poor health— long the lot of much of humanity, and still the fate of an outrageously high proportion of the world today."[98]

Back in the days of the early Progressive movement at the beginning of the twentieth century, John Dewey questioned whether most people even cared much about freedom, in the sense the word meant for centuries before Woodrow Wilson redefined it. Dewey said:

> Does freedom in itself and in the things it brings with it seem as important as security of livelihood; as food, shelter, clothing, or even as having a good time?[99]

Dewey asked, "how does the desire for freedom compare in intensity with the desire to feel equal with others, especially with those who have previously been called superiors?"[100] He said, "as we look at the world we see supposedly free institutions in many countries not so much overthrown as abandoned willingly, apparently with enthusiasm."[101]

Although Dewey was a professor of philosophy, well aware that theories "must be regarded as hypotheses" to be subjected to "actions which test them," so that they are not to be accepted as "rigid dogmas,"[102] no such tests or evidence accompanied his own sweeping pronouncements about such things as "obvious social evils" in contemporary American society.[103] Nor were such tests applied to Professor Dewey's other sweeping pronouncements about "our defective industrial regime,"[104] his claim that "Industrial entrepreneurs have reaped out of all proportion to what they sowed,"[105] or that schools needed to offset "the coarseness, blunders, and prejudices of their elders" that children see at home.[106]

This casual contempt for ordinary people and their freedom was by no means confined to John Dewey, or to educators. In the law as well, there has been the same disregard of other people's rights and values by intellectual elites. One of the leading legal authorities of the Progressive era was Roscoe Pound, who was for 20 years— from 1916 to 1936— Dean of the Harvard Law School, which turned out many leading legal scholars promoting an expansive role for judges in "interpreting" the Constitution to loosen its restrictions on government power, in the cause of what Roscoe Pound called "social justice," as far back as 1907.[107]

Pound invoked the words "science" and "scientific" repeatedly in his discussions,[108] which had neither the procedures nor the precision of science. There was to be a "science of politics,"[109] and a "science of law."[110] Similarly, Pound repeatedly called for "social engineering,"[111] as if other human beings were to be like inert components of social machinery, to be constructed by elites into a society with "social justice."

With Pound, as with Woodrow Wilson, what the public at large wanted faded into the background. Pound lamented that "we still harp upon the sacredness of property before the law" and approvingly cited the "progress of law away from the older individualism" which "is not confined to property rights."[112]

Thus, in 1907 and 1908, Roscoe Pound set forth principles of judicial activism— going beyond interpreting the law to making social policy— that would still be dominant, more than a hundred years later, and on into the present. One of the rationales for such an expanded role for judges has been the claim that the Constitution is too hard to amend, so that judges must amend it by "interpretation," to adapt it to changing times.

Like so much that has been said and repeated endlessly by elites with the social justice vision, this rationale is contradicted by readily available facts. The Constitution of the United States was amended *4 times in 8 years*— from 1913 through 1920[113]— during the heyday of the Progressives, who claimed that it was nearly impossible to amend the Constitution.[114] When the people wanted the Constitution amended, it was amended. When the elites wanted it amended, but the people did not, that was not a "problem" to be "solved." That was democracy, even if it frustrated elites convinced that their superior wisdom and virtue should be imposed on others.

Dean Pound simply dismissed as "dogma" the Constitution's separation of powers, because the separation of powers would "limit the courts to interpretation and application" of the law.[115] Pound's own conception of the role of judges was far more expansive.

As far back as 1908, Pound referred to the desirability of "a living constitution by judicial interpretation."[116] He called for "an awakening of juristic activity," for "the sociological jurist," and declared that law "must be judged by the results it achieves."[117] What he called "mechanical" jurisprudence[118] was condemned for "its failure to respond to vital needs of present-day life." When law "becomes a body of rules," that "is the condition against which sociologists now protest, and protest rightly,"[119] he said. Why judges and sociologists should be making social policy, instead of people elected as legislators or executives, was not explained.

Whether in law or in other areas, one of the hallmarks of elite intellectuals' seeking to preempt other people's decisions— whether on public policy or in their own private lives— is a reliance on unsubstantiated *pronouncements*, based on elite consensus, treated as if that was equivalent to documented facts. One revealing sign of this is how often the arguments of people with other views are not answered with counter-arguments, but with *ad hominem* assertions instead. This pattern has persisted for more than a century, not only in discussions of social justice issues, but also in other issues— and not only in the United States, but also among other intellectual elites in countries on the other side of the Atlantic.

From the earliest days of the Progressive era in the United States, one of the features of Progressives' conceptions of advanced social thinking was that automatic punishment of criminals should be replaced, or at least supplemented, by *treatment* of the criminal, as if crime were a disease— and a disease whose "root causes" could be traced to society, as well as to the criminal. Such ideas can be traced back at least as far as such eighteenth-century writers as William Godwin in England and the Marquis de Condorcet in France.[120] But these ideas were often presented by twentieth-century Progressives as new revelations of modern "social science" and were widely celebrated among intellectual elites.[121]

In this atmosphere, the Supreme Court of the United States, in a series of early 1960s cases, began to "interpret" the Constitution as providing newly discovered "rights" for criminals that had apparently escaped notice before. These cases included *Mapp v. Ohio* (1961), *Escobedo v. Illinois* (1964) and *Miranda v. Arizona* (1966). The Supreme Court majority, led by Chief Justice Earl Warren, were undeterred by bitter dissenting opinions from other Justices, who objected to both the dangers being created and the lack of legal basis for the decisions.[122]

At a 1965 conference of judges and legal scholars, when a former police commissioner complained about the trend of recent Supreme Court decisions on criminal law, Justice William J. Brennan and Chief Justice Earl Warren sat "stony-faced" during his presentation, according to a *New York Times* account. But, after a law professor responded with scorn and ridicule to what the commissioner said, Warren and Brennan "frequently roared with laughter."[123]

A mere police official opposing learned Olympians of the law may have seemed humorous to elites at this gathering. But some crime statistics might present a somewhat different perspective. Prior to the Supreme Court's remaking of the criminal law, beginning in the early 1960s, the homicide rate in the United States had been going down for three consecutive decades— and that rate, in proportion to population, was in 1960 just under *half* of what it had been in 1934.[124] But almost immediately after the Supreme Court's creation of sweeping new "rights" for criminals, the homicide rate reversed. It *doubled* from 1963 to 1973.[125]

No one found that humorous, least of all the mothers, widows and orphans of homicide victims. Although this was a nationwide trend, it was especially severe in black communities— places supposedly being helped by social justice advocates, who were often also advocates of a de-emphasis of law enforcement and punishment, seeking instead to treat the "root causes" of crime.

Both before and after the 1960s sudden upsurge in homicides, the homicide *rate* among blacks was consistently some multiple of the homicide rate among whites. In some years there were more black homicide victims than white homicide victims— in absolute numbers[126]— even though the size of the black population was only a fraction of the size of the white population. This meant that the sudden upsurge in homicides took an especially heavy toll in black communities.

Supreme Court Justices with lifetime tenure are classic examples of elites who institutionally *pay no price for being wrong*— no matter how wrong, and no matter how high the price paid by others. Chief Justice Earl Warren did not even pay the price of admitting a mistake. In his memoirs, he rejected critics of the Supreme Court's criminal law decisions. He blamed crime "in our disturbed society" on "the root causes" of crime— citing such examples as "poverty," "unemployment," and "the degradation of slum life."[127] But he offered no factual evidence that any of these things had suddenly gotten worse in the 1960s than they had been in the three preceding decades, when the homicide rate was going down.

IMPLICATIONS

How we see the distribution of consequential knowledge is crucial for deciding what kinds of decisions make sense, through what kinds of policies and institutions. We each have our own island of knowledge in a sea of ignorance. Some islands are larger than others, but no island is as large as the sea. As Hayek conceived it, the enormously vast amount of consequential knowledge dispersed among the population of a whole society makes the differences in the amount of such knowledge between some people and other people "comparatively insignificant."[128]

This conclusion provides little basis for intellectual elites to engage in wholesale preemption of other people's decisions, whether these are decisions about how they live their own lives or decisions about the kinds of laws the voting public want to live under, and the people they want in charge of carrying out those laws. Intellectual elites with outstanding achievements within their own respective specialties may give little thought to how ignorant they may be on a vast spectrum of other concerns.

Even more dangerous than ignorance, however, is a fallacious certitude, which can afflict people at all educational levels and all IQ levels. While we may not see our own fallacies, the saving grace in this situation is that we can often see other people's fallacies much more clearly— and they can see ours. In a world of inevitably fallible human beings, with inevitably different viewpoints and different fragments of consequential knowledge, our ability to correct each other can be essential to preventing our making fatally dangerous mistakes as individuals, or as a society.

The fatal danger of our times today is a growing intolerance and suppression of both opinions and evidence that differ from the prevailing ideologies that dominate institutions, ranging from the academic world to the corporate world, the media and governmental institutions.

Many intellectuals with high accomplishments seem to assume that those accomplishments confer validity to their notions about a broad swath of issues, ranging far beyond the scope of their accomplishments. But stepping outside the scope of one's expertise can be like stepping off a cliff.

A high IQ and low information can be a very dangerous combination, as a basis for preempting other people's decisions— especially when this preemption takes place in circumstances where there is no price for surrogate decision-makers to pay for being wrong.

Stupid people can create problems, but it often takes brilliant people to create a real catastrophe. They have already done that enough times— and in enough different ways— for us to reconsider, before joining their latest stampedes, led by self-congratulatory elites, deaf to argument and immune to evidence.

Chapter 5

WORDS, DEEDS AND DANGERS

> . . .we must be aware of the dangers which
> lie in our most generous wishes.
>
> Lionel Trilling[1]

People who may share many of the same basic concerns that social justice advocates have do not necessarily share the same vision or agenda, because they do not make the same assumptions about options, causation or consequences. Iconic free-market economist Milton Friedman, for example, said:

> Everywhere in the world there are gross inequities of income and wealth. They offend most of us. Few can fail to be moved by the contrast between the luxury enjoyed by some and the grinding poverty suffered by others.[2]

Similarly, F.A. Hayek— another iconic free-market economist— said:

> It has of course to be admitted that the manner in which the benefits and burdens are apportioned by the market mechanism would in many instances have to be regarded as very unjust *if* it were the result of a deliberate allocation to particular people.[3]

Clearly, Hayek also saw life in general as unfair, even with the free markets he advocated. But that is not the same as saying that he saw *society* as unfair. To Hayek, society was "an orderly structure," but not a decision-making unit, or an institution taking action.[4] That is what *governments* do.[5] But neither society nor government comprehends or controls all the many and highly varied circumstances— including a large element of luck— that can influence the fate of individuals, classes, races or nations.

Even within the same family, as we have seen, it matters whether you were the first-born child or the last-born child. When the first-born child in five-child families constituted 52 percent of the children from such families to become National Merit Scholarship finalists, while the fifth-born child in those families became the finalist just 6 percent of the time,[6] that is a disparity larger than most disparities between the sexes or the races.

In a growing economy, it also matters which generation of the family you were born into.[7] A facetious headline in *The Economist* magazine— "Choose your parents wisely"[8]— highlighted another important truth about inequalities, illustrated with this impossible advice. Circumstances beyond our control are major factors in economic and other inequalities. Trying to understand causation is not necessarily the same as looking for someone to blame.

The totality of circumstances around us Hayek called a "cosmos"[9] or universe. In this context, what others call "social justice" might more fittingly be called "*cosmic* justice,"[10] since that is what would be required to produce the results sought by many social justice advocates.

This is not simply a question about different names. It is a more fundamental question about what we can and cannot do— and at what costs and risks. When there are "differences in human fates for which clearly no human agency is responsible,"[11] as Hayek put it, we cannot demand justice from the cosmos. No human beings, either singly or collectively, can control the cosmos— that is, the whole universe of circumstances surrounding us and affecting everyone's chances in life. The large element of luck in all our lives means that neither society nor government has either causal control or moral responsibility extending to everything that has gone right or wrong in everybody's life.

Some of us may be able to think of some particular individual, whose appearance in our lives at one particular juncture altered the trajectory of our lives. There may be more than one such person, at different stages of our lives, who changed our prospects in different ways, for better or worse. Neither we nor surrogate decision-makers control such things. Those who imagine that they can— that they are either a "self-made man" or surrogate saviors of other people or the planet— operate in dangerous territory, littered with human tragedies and national catastrophes.

If the world around us happened to provide equal chances for all people in all endeavors— whether as individuals or as classes, races or nations— that might well be seen as a world far superior to the world we actually see around us today. Whether called social justice or cosmic justice, that might be seen as ideal by many people who agree on little else. But our ideals tell us nothing about our capabilities and their limits— or the dangers of trying to go beyond those limits.

As just one example, from the earliest American Progressives onward, there has been an ideal of applying criminal laws in a manner individualized to the criminal, rather than generalized from the crime.[12] Before even considering whether this is desirable, there is first the question of whether human beings are even *capable* of doing such a thing. Where would officials acquire such sweeping, intimate and accurate knowledge about a stranger, much less have the superhuman wisdom to apply it in the incalculable complications of life?

A murderer may have had an unhappy childhood, but does that justify gambling other people's lives, by turning him loose among them, after some process that has been given the name "rehabilitation"? Are high-sounding notions and fashionable catchwords important enough to risk the lives of innocent men, women and children?

F.A. Hayek's key insight was that all the consequential knowledge essential to the functioning of a large society exists in its totality *nowhere* in any given individual, class or institution. Therefore the functioning and survival of a large society requires coordination among innumerable people with innumerable fragments of consequential knowledge. This put Hayek in opposition to various systems of centrally directed control, whether a centrally planned economy, systems of comprehensive surrogate decision-making in the interests of social justice, or presumptions of "society" being morally responsible for all its inhabitants' good or bad fates, when nobody has the requisite knowledge for such responsibility.

The fact that we cannot do everything does not mean that we should do nothing. But it does suggest that we need to make very sure that we have our facts straight, so that we do not make things worse, while trying to make them better. In a world of ever-changing facts and inherently fallible human beings, that means leaving everything we say or do be open to criticism. Dogmatic certitudes and intolerance of dissent have often led to major catastrophes, and nowhere more so than in the twentieth century. The continuation and escalation of such practices in the twenty-first century is by no means a hopeful sign.

Back in the eighteenth century, Edmund Burke made a fundamental distinction between his ideals and his policy advocacies. "Preserving my principles unshaken," he said, "I reserve my activity for rational endeavours."[13] In other words, having high ideals did not imply carrying ideal*ism* to the extreme of trying to impose those ideals *at all costs* and oblivious to all dangers.

Pursuing high ideals at all costs has already been tried, especially in twentieth-century creations of totalitarian dictatorships, often based on egalitarian goals with the highest moral principles. But powers conferred for the finest reasons can be used for the worst purposes— and, beyond some point, powers conferred cannot be taken back. Milton Friedman clearly understood this:

> A society that puts equality— in the sense of equality of outcome— ahead of freedom will end up with neither equality nor freedom. The use of force to achieve equality will destroy freedom, and the force, introduced for good purposes, will end up in the hands of people who use it to promote their own interests.[14]

F.A. Hayek— having lived through the era of the rise of totalitarian dictatorships in twentieth-century Europe— and having witnessed how it happened— arrived at essentially the same conclusions. But he did not regard social justice advocates as evil people, plotting to create totalitarian dictatorships. Hayek said that some of the leading advocates of social justice included individuals whose unselfishness was "beyond question."[15]

Hayek's argument was that the kind of world idealized by social justice advocates— a world with everyone having equal chances of success in all endeavors— was not only unattainable, but that its fervent but futile pursuit can lead to the opposite of what its advocates are seeking. It was not that social justice advocates would create dictatorships, but that their passionate attacks on existing democracies could weaken those democracies to the point where *others* could seize dictatorial powers.

Social justice advocates themselves obviously do not share the conclusions of their critics, such as Friedman and Hayek. But the differences in their conclusions are not necessarily differences in fundamental moral values. Their differences tend to be at the level of fundamentally *different beliefs about circumstances* and *assumptions about causation* that can produce very different conclusions. They envision different worlds, operating on different principles, and describe these worlds with words that have different meanings within the framework of different visions.

When visions and vocabularies differ so fundamentally, an examination of facts offers at least a hope of clarification.

VISIONS AND VOCABULARIES

In a sense, words are just the containers in which meanings are conveyed from some people to other people. But, like some other containers, words can sometimes contaminate their contents. A word like "merit," for example, varies in its meanings. As a result, this word has contaminated many discussions of social policies, whether it has been used by advocates or critics of the social justice vision.

Merit

Opponents of group preferences, such as affirmative action for hiring or for college admissions, often say that each individual should be judged by that individual's own *merit*. In most cases, "merit" in this context seems to mean individual capabilities that are relevant to the particular endeavor. Merit in this sense is simply a factual question, and the validity of the answer depends on the predictive validity of the criteria used to compare different applicants' capabilities.

Others, however— including social justice advocates— see not only a factual issue, but also a *moral* issue, in the concept of merit. As far back as the eighteenth century, social justice advocate William Godwin was concerned not only about unequal outcomes, but especially "unmerited advantage."[16] Twentieth-century Fabian socialist pioneer George Bernard Shaw likewise said that "enormous fortunes are made without the least merit."[17] He noted that not only the poor, but also many well-educated people, "see successful men of business, inferior to themselves in knowledge, talent, character, and public spirit, making much larger incomes."[18]

Here merit is no longer simply a factual question about who has the particular capabilities relevant to success in a particular endeavor. There is now also a *moral* question as to how those capabilities were acquired— whether they were a result of some special personal exertions or were just some "unmerited advantage," perhaps due to being born into unusually more favorable circumstances than the circumstances of most other people.

Merit in this sense, with a moral dimension, raises very different questions, which can have very different answers. Do people born into certain German families or certain German communities *deserve* to inherit the benefits of the knowledge, experience and insights derived from more than a thousand years of Germans brewing beer? Clearly, they do not! It is a windfall gain. But, equally clearly, their possession of this valuable knowledge is a fact of life today, whether we like it or not. Nor is this kind of situation peculiar to Germans or to beer.

It so happens that the first black American to become a general in the U.S. Air Force— General Benjamin O. Davis, Jr.— was the son of the first black American to become a general in the U.S. Army, General Benjamin O. Davis, Sr. Did other black Americans— or white Americans, for that matter— have the same advantage of growing up in a military family, automatically learning, from childhood onward, about the many aspects of a career as a senior military officer?

Nor was this situation unique. One of the most famous American generals in World War II— and one of the most famous in American military history— was General Douglas MacArthur. His father was a young commanding officer in the Civil War, where his performance on the battlefield brought him the Congressional Medal of Honor. He ended his long military career as a general.

None of this is peculiar to the military. In the National Football League, quarterback Archie Manning had a long and distinguished career, in which he threw more than a hundred touchdown passes.[19] His sons— Peyton Manning and Eli Manning— also had long and distinguished careers as NFL quarterbacks, which in their cases included winning Super Bowls. Did other quarterbacks, not having a father who had been an NFL quarterback before them, have equal chances? Not very likely. But would football fans rather watch other quarterbacks who were not as good, but who had been chosen in order to equalize social justice?

The advantages that some people have, in a given endeavor, are not just disadvantages to everyone else. These advantages also benefit all the people who pay for the product or service provided by that endeavor. It is *not* a zero-sum situation. Mutual benefit is the only way the endeavor can continue, in a competitive market, with vast numbers of people free to decide what they are willing to pay for. The losers are the much smaller number of people who wanted to supply the same product or service. But the losers were unable to match what the successful producers offered, regardless of whether the winners' success was due to skills developed at great sacrifice or skills that came their way from just happening to be in the right place at the right time.

When computer-based products spread around the world, both their producers and their consumers benefitted. It was bad news for manufacturers of competing products such as typewriters, or the slide rules that were once standard equipment used by engineers for making mathematical calculations. Small computerized devices could make those calculations faster, simpler and with a vastly larger range of applications. But, in a free-market economy, progress based on new advances inevitably means bad news for those whose goods or services are no longer the best. Demographic "inclusion" requires some surrogate decision-makers, empowered to over-rule what consumers want.

A similar situation exists in the military. A country fighting for its life, on the battlefield, cannot afford the luxury of choosing its generals on the basis of demographic representation— "looking like America"— rather than on the basis of military skills, regardless of how those skills were acquired. Not if the country wants to win and survive. That is especially so if the country wants to win its military victories without more losses of soldiers' lives than necessary. In that case, it cannot put generals in charge of those soldiers when these are not the best generals available.

In the social justice literature, unmerited advantages tend to be treated as if they are *deductions* from the well-being of the rest of the population. But there is no fixed or predestined amount of well-being, whether measured in financial terms or in terms of spectators enjoying a sport, or soldiers surviving a battle. When President Barack Obama said: "The top 10 percent no longer takes in one-third of our income, it now takes half,"[20] that would clearly be a deduction from other people's incomes *if there were a fixed or predestined amount of total income.*

This is not an incidental subtlety. *It matters greatly whether people with high incomes are adding to, or subtracting from, the incomes of the rest of the population.* Insinuations are a weak basis for making decisions about a serious issue. It is too important to have that issue decided— or obfuscated— by artful words. In plain English: Is the average American's income higher or lower because of the products created and sold by some multi-billionaire?

Again, there is no fixed or predestined total amount of income or wealth to be shared. If some people are creating more wealth than they are receiving as income, then they are *not* making other people poorer. But if they are creating products or services that are worth less than the income they receive, then equally clearly they *are* making other people poorer. But, although anyone can charge any price they want to, for whatever they are selling, they are not likely to find people who will pay more than the product or service is worth to themselves.

Arguing as if some people's high incomes were deducted from some fixed or predestined total income— leaving less for others— may be clever. But cleverness is not wisdom, and artful insinuations are no substitute for factual evidence, *if* your goal is knowing the facts. But, if your goals are political or ideological, there is no question that one of the most politically successful messages of the twentieth century was that the rich have gotten rich by taking from the poor.

The Marxian message of "exploitation" helped sweep communists into power in countries around the world in the twentieth century, at a pace and on a scale seldom seen in history. There is clearly a political market for that message, and communists are just one of the ideological groups to use it successfully for their own purposes, despite how disastrously that turned out to be for millions of other human beings living under communist dictatorships.

The very possibility that poor Americans, for example, are having a rising standard of living *because of progress created by people who are getting rich*— as suggested by Herman Kahn[21]— would be anathema to social justice advocates. But it is by no means obvious that empirical tests of that hypothesis would vindicate those who advocate social justice. It seems even less likely that social justice advocates would put that hypothesis to an empirical test.

For people seeking facts, rather than political or ideological goals, there are many factual tests that might be applied, in order to see if the wealth of the wealthy is derived from the poverty of the poor. One way might be to see if countries with many billionaires— either absolutely or relative to the size of the population— have higher or lower standards of living among the rest of their people. The United States, for example, has more billionaires than there are in the entire continent of Africa plus the Middle East.[22] But even Americans living in conditions officially defined as poverty usually have a higher standard of living than that of most of the people in Africa and the Middle East.

Other factual tests might include examining the history of prosperous ethnic minorities, who have often been depicted as "exploiters" in various times and places over the years. Such minorities have, in many cases over the years, been either expelled by governments or driven out of particular cities or countries by mob violence, or both. This has happened to Jews a number of times over the centuries in various parts of Europe.[23] The overseas Chinese have had similar experiences in various southeast Asian countries.[24] So have Indians and Pakistanis expelled from Uganda in East Africa.[25] So have the Chettiar money-lenders in

Burma, after that country's laws confiscating much of their property in 1948, drove many of them out of Burma.[26]

The Ugandan economy collapsed in the 1970s, after the government expelled Asian business owners,[27] who had supposedly been making Africans worse off economically. Interest rates in Burma went *up*, not down, after the Chettiars were gone.[28] It was much the same story in the Philippines, where 23,000 overseas Chinese were massacred in the seventeenth century, after which there were shortages of the goods produced by the Chinese.[29]

In centuries past, it was not uncommon for Jews in Europe to be driven out— denounced as "exploiters" and "bloodsuckers"— from various cities and countries, whether forced out by government edict or mob violence, or both. What is remarkable is how often Jews were in later years *invited back* to some of the places from which they had been expelled.[30]

Apparently some of those who drove them out discovered that the country was worse off economically after the Jews were gone.

Although Catherine the Great banned Jews from immigrating into Russia, in her later efforts to attract much-needed foreign skills from Western Europe, including "some merchant people," she wrote to one of her officials that people in the occupations being sought should be given passports to Russia, "not mentioning their nationality and without enquiring into their confession." To the formal Russian text of this message she added a postscript in German saying, "If you don't understand me, it will not be my fault" and "keep all this secret."[31]

In the wake of this message, Jews began to be recruited as immigrants to Russia— even though, as a historian has noted, "throughout the whole transaction any reference to Jewishness was scrupulously avoided."[32] In short, even despotic rulers may seek to evade their own policies, when it is impolitic to repeal those policies, and counterproductive to follow them.

These historical events are by no means the only factual tests that could be used to determine whether more prosperous people are making other people less prosperous. Nor are these necessarily the best factual tests. But the far larger point is that a prevailing social vision does not have to produce *any* factual test, when rhetoric and repetition can be sufficient to accomplish their aims, especially when alternative views can be ignored and/or suppressed. It is that suppression which is a key factor— and it is already a large and growing factor in academic, political and other institutions in our own times.

Today it is possible, even in our most prestigious educational institutions at all levels, to go literally from kindergarten to a Ph.D., without ever having read a single article— much less a book— by someone who advocates free-market economies or who opposes gun control laws. Whether you would agree with them or disagree with them, if you read what they said, is not the issue. The far larger issue is why education has so often become indoctrination— and for whose benefit.

The issue is not even whether what is being indoctrinated is true or false. Even if we were to assume, for the sake of argument, that everything with which students are being indoctrinated today is true, these issues of today are by no means necessarily the same as the issues that are likely to arise during the half-century or more of life that most students have ahead of them after they have finished their education. What good would it do them then, to have the right answers to yesterday's questions?

What they will need then, in order to sort out the new controversial issues, is an education that has equipped them with the intellectual skills, knowledge and experience to confront and analyze opposing views— and subject those views to scrutiny and systematic analysis. That is precisely what they do *not* get when being indoctrinated with whatever is currently in vogue today.

Such "education" sets up whole generations to become easy prey for whatever clever demagogues come along, with heady rhetoric that can manipulate people's emotions. As John Stuart Mill put the issue, long ago:

> He who knows only his own side of the case, knows little of that. . .
> Nor is it enough that he should hear the arguments of adversaries from his own teachers, presented as they state them, and accompanied by what they offer as refutations. That is not the way to do justice to the arguments, or bring them into real contact with his own mind. He must be able to hear them from persons who actually believe

them; who defend them in earnest, and do their very utmost for
them. He must know them in their most plausible and persuasive
form. . .[33]

What Mill described is precisely what most students today do *not*
get, in even our most prestigious educational institutions. What they are
more likely to get are prepackaged conclusions, wrapped securely against
the intrusion of other ideas— or of facts inconsistent with the prevailing
narratives.

In the prevailing narratives of our time, someone else's good luck is
your bad luck— and a "problem" to be "solved." But when someone has,
however undeservedly, acquired some knowledge and insights that can
be used to design a product which enables billions of people around the
world to use computers— without knowing anything about the specifics
of computer science— that is a product which can, over the years, add
trillions of dollars' worth of wealth to the world's existing supply of
wealth. If the producer of that product becomes a multi-billionaire by
selling it to those billions of people, that does not make those people
poorer.

People like British socialist George Bernard Shaw may lament that
the producer of this product may not have either the academic credentials
or the personal virtues which Shaw seems to attribute to himself, and to
others like himself. But that is not what the buyers of the computerized
product are paying for, with their own money. Nor is it obvious why a
third-party's laments should be allowed to affect transactions which are
not doing the third party any harm. Nor is the general track record of
third-party preemptions encouraging.

None of this suggests that businesses have never done anything
wrong. Sainthood is not the norm in business, any more than in politics,
in the media or on academic campuses. That is why we have laws. But
it is not a reason to create ever more numerous and sweeping laws to
put ever more power in the hands of people who pay no price for being
wrong, regardless of how high a price is paid by others who are subject
to their power.

Slippery words like "merit"— with multiple and conflicting meanings— can make it hard to clearly understand what the issues are, much less see how to resolve them.

Racism

"Racism" may be the most powerful word in the social justice vocabulary. There is no question that racism has inflicted an enormous amount of needless suffering on innocent people, punctuated by unspeakable horrors, such as the Holocaust.

Racism might be analogized to some deadly pandemic disease. If so, it may be worth considering the consequences of responding to pandemics in different ways. We certainly cannot simply ignore the disease and hope for the best. But we cannot go to the opposite extreme, and sacrifice every other concern— including other deadly diseases— in hopes of reducing fatalities from the pandemic. During the Covid-19 pandemic, for example, death rates from *other* diseases went up,[34] because many people feared going to medical facilities, where they might catch Covid from other patients.

Even the most terrible pandemics can subside or end. At some point, continued preoccupation with the pandemic disease can then cause more dangers and death from other diseases, and from other life stresses resulting from continued restrictions that may have made sense when the pandemic was in full force, but are counterproductive on net balance afterwards.

Everything depends on what the specific facts are at a given time and place. That is not always easy to know. It may be especially difficult to know, when special interests have benefitted politically or financially from the pandemic restrictions, and therefore have every incentive to promote the belief that those restrictions are still urgently needed.

Similarly, it can be especially hard to know about the current incidence and consequences of racism, when racists do not publicly identify themselves. Moreover, people who have incentives to maximize fears of racism include politicians seeking to win votes by claiming to offer protection from racists, or leaders of ethnic protest movements who can use fears of racists to attract more followers, more donations and more power.

No sane person believes that there is zero racism in American society, or in any other society. Here it may be worth recalling what Edmund Burke said, back in the eighteenth century: "Preserving my principles unshaken, I reserve my activity for rational endeavours."[35] Our principles can reject racism completely. But neither a racial minority nor anyone else has unlimited time, unlimited energy or unlimited resources to invest in seeking out every possible trace of racism— or to invest in the even less promising activity of trying to morally enlighten racists.

Even if, by some miracle, we could get to zero racism, we already know, from the history of American hillbillies— who are physically indistinguishable from other white people, and therefore face zero racism— that even this is not enough to prevent poverty. Meanwhile, black married-couple families, who are *not* exempt from racism, have nevertheless had poverty rates in single digits, every year for more than a quarter of a century.[36] We also know that racists today cannot prevent black young people from becoming pilots in the Air Force, or even generals in the Air Force, nor from becoming millionaires, billionaires or President of the United States.

Just as we need to recognize when the power of a pandemic has at least subsided, so that we can use more of our limited time, energy and resources against other dangers, so we also need to pay more attention to other dangers besides racism. That is especially so for the younger generation, who need to deal with the problems and dangers actually confronting them, rather than remain fixated on the problems and dangers of the generations before them. *If racists cannot prevent today's minority young people from becoming pilots, the teachers unions can—* by denying them a decent education, in schools whose top priorities are iron-clad job security for teachers, and billions of dollars in union dues for teachers unions.[37]

It is by no means certain whether the enemies of American minorities are able to do them as much harm as their supposed "friends" and "benefactors." We have already seen some of the harm that minimum wage laws have done, by denying black teenagers the option of taking jobs that employers are willing to offer, at pay that teenagers are willing to accept, because unaffected third parties choose to believe that they understand the situation better than all the people directly involved.

Another "benefit" for minorities, from those with the social justice vision and agenda, is "affirmative action." This is an issue often discussed in terms of the harm done to people who would have gotten particular jobs, college admissions or other benefits, if these had been awarded on the basis of qualifications, rather than demographic representation. But the harm done to the supposed beneficiaries also needs to be understood— and that harm can be even worse.

This possibility especially needs to be examined, because it goes completely counter to the prevailing social justice agenda and its narrative about the sources of black Americans' advancement. In that narrative, blacks' rise out of poverty was due to the civil rights laws and social welfare policies of the 1960s, including affirmative action. An empirical test of that narrative is long overdue.

Affirmative Action

In the prevailing narrative on the socioeconomic progress of black Americans, statistical data have been cited, showing declining proportions of the black population living in poverty after the 1960s, and rising proportions of the black population employed in professional occupations, as well as having rising incomes. But, as with many other statements about statistical trends over time, the arbitrary choice of which year to select as the beginning of the statistical evaluation can be crucial in determining the validity of the conclusions.

If the statistical data on the annual rate of poverty among black Americans were to be presented, beginning in 1940— that is, 20 years *before* the civil rights laws and expanded social welfare state policies of the 1960s— the conclusions are very different.

These data show that the poverty rate among blacks fell from 87 percent in 1940 to 47 percent over the next two decades[38]— that is, *before* the major civil rights laws and social welfare policies of the 1960s. This trend continued after the 1960s, but did not originate then and did not accelerate then. The poverty rate among blacks fell an additional 17 points, to 30 percent in 1970— a rate only slightly lower than that in the two preceding decades, but certainly not higher. The black poverty rate fell yet again during the 1970s, from 30 percent in 1970 to 29 percent in 1980.[39] This one-percentage-point decline in poverty was clearly much less than in the three preceding decades.

Where does affirmative action fit in with this history? The first use of the phrase "affirmative action" in a Presidential Executive Order was by President John F. Kennedy in 1961. That Executive Order said that federal contractors should "take affirmative action to ensure that applicants are employed, and that employees are treated during employment, without regard to their race, creed, color, or national origin."[40] In other words, at that point affirmative action meant equal opportunity for individuals, *not* equal outcomes for groups. Subsequent Executive Orders by Presidents Lyndon B. Johnson and Richard Nixon made numerical group outcomes the test of affirmative action by the 1970s.

With affirmative action now transformed from equal individual opportunity to equalized group outcomes, many people saw this as a more beneficial policy for blacks and other low-income racial or ethnic groups to whom this principle applied. Indeed, it was widely regarded as axiomatic that this would better promote their progress in many areas. But the one-percentage-point decline in black poverty during the 1970s, after affirmative action meant group preferences or quotas, goes completely counter to the prevailing narrative.

Over the years, as controversies raged about affirmative action as group preferences, the prevailing narrative defended affirmative action as a major contributor to black progress. As with many other controversial issues, however, a consensus of elite opinion has been widely accepted, with little recourse to vast amounts of empirical evidence to the contrary. Best-selling author Shelby Steele, whose incisive books have explored the rationales and incentives behind support for failed social policies,[41] cited an encounter he had with a man who had been a government official involved in the 1960s policies:

> "Look," he said irritably, "*only*— and I mean *only*— the government
> can get to that kind of poverty, that entrenched, deep poverty. And

> I don't care what you say. If this country was decent, it would let the
> government try again."[42]

Professor Steele's attempt to focus on facts about the actual
consequences of various government programs of the 1960s brought a
heated response:

> "Damn it, we *saved* this country!" he all but shouted. "This country
> was about to blow up. There were riots everywhere. You can stand
> there now in hindsight and criticize, but we had to keep the country
> together, my friend."[43]

From a factual standpoint, this former 1960s official had the
sequence completely wrong. Nor was he unique in that. The massive
ghetto riots across the nation began *during* the Lyndon Johnson
administration, on a scale unseen before.[44] The riots subsided after
that administration ended, and its "war on poverty" programs were
repudiated by the next administration. Still later, during the eight years
of the Reagan administration, which rejected that whole approach,
there were no such massive waves of riots.

Of course politicians have every incentive to depict black progress
as something for which politicians can take credit. So do social justice
advocates, who supported these policies. But that narrative enables
some critics to complain that blacks ought to lift themselves out of
poverty, as other groups have done. Yet the cold facts demonstrate that
this is largely what blacks did, during decades when blacks did not yet
have even equal opportunity, much less group preferences.

These were decades when neither the federal government, the
media, nor intellectual elites paid anything like the amount of attention
to blacks that they did from the 1960s on. As for the attention paid to
blacks by governments in Southern states during the 1940s and 1950s,
that was largely negative, in accordance with the racially discriminatory
laws and policies at that time.

Among the ways by which many blacks escaped from poverty in
the 1940s and 1950s was migrating out of the South, gaining better
economic opportunities for adults and better education for their

children.[45] The Civil Rights Act of 1964 was an overdue major factor in ending the denial of basic Constitutional rights to blacks in the South.[46] But there is no point trying to make that also the main source of the black rise out of poverty. The rate of rise of blacks into the professions more than doubled from 1954 to 1964[47]— that is, *before* the historic Civil Rights Act of 1964. Nor can the political left act as if the Civil Rights Act of 1964 was solely their work. The *Congressional Record* shows that a higher percentage of Republicans than Democrats voted for that Act.[48]

In short, during the decades when the rise of black Americans out of poverty was greatest, the causes of that rise were most like the causes of the rise of other low-income groups in the United States, and in other countries around the world. That is, it was primarily a result of the individual decisions of millions of ordinary people, on their own initiative, and owed little to charismatic group leaders, to government programs, to intellectual elites or to media publicity. It is doubtful if most Americans of that earlier era even knew the names of leaders of the most prominent civil rights organizations of that era.

Affirmative action in the United States, like similar group preference policies in other countries, seldom provided much benefit for people in poverty.[49] A typical teenager in a low-income minority community in the United States, having usually gotten a very poor education in such neighborhoods, is unlikely to be able to make use of preferential admissions to medical schools, when it would be a major challenge just to graduate from an ordinary college. In a much poorer country, such as India, it could be an even bigger challenge for a rural youngster from one of the "scheduled castes"— formerly known as "untouchables."[50]

Both in the United States and in other countries with group preference policies, benefits created for poorer groups have often gone disproportionately to the more prosperous members of these poorer groups[51]— and sometimes to people more prosperous than the average member of the larger society.[52]

The central premise of affirmative action is that group "under-representation" is the problem, and proportional representation of groups is the solution. This might make sense if all segments of a society had equal capabilities in all endeavors. But neither social justice advocates, nor anyone else, seems able to come up with an example of any such society today, or in the thousands of years of recorded history. Even highly successful groups have seldom been highly successful in all endeavors. Asian Americans and Jewish Americans are seldom found among the leading athletic stars or German Americans among charismatic politicians.

At the very least, it is worth considering such basic facts as the extent to which affirmative action has been beneficial or harmful, on net balance, for those it was designed to help— in a world where specific developed capabilities are seldom equal, even when reciprocal inequalities are common. One example is the widespread practice of admitting members of low-income minority groups to colleges and universities under less stringent requirements than other students have to meet.

Such affirmative action in college admissions policies has been widely justified on the ground that few students educated in the public schools in low-income minority neighborhoods have the kind of test scores that would get them admitted to top-level colleges and universities otherwise. So group preferences in admissions are thought to be a solution.

Despite the implicit assumption that students will get a better education at a higher-ranked institution, there are serious reasons to doubt it. Professors tend to teach at a pace, and at a level of complexity, appropriate for the particular kinds of students they are teaching. A student who is fully qualified to be admitted to many good quality colleges or universities can nevertheless be overwhelmed by the pace and complexity of courses taught at an elite institution, where most of the students score in the top ten percent nationwide— or even the top one percent— on the mathematics and verbal parts of the Scholastic Aptitude Test (SAT).

Admitting a student who scores at the 80th percentile to such an institution, because that student is a member of a minority group, is no favor. It can turn someone who is fully qualified for success into a frustrated failure. An intelligent student who scored at the 80th percentile in mathematics can find the pace of math courses far too fast to keep up with, while the professor's brief explanations of complex principles may be readily understood by the other students in the class, who scored at the 99th percentile. They may already have learned half this material in high school. It can be much the same story with the amount and complexity of readings assigned to students in an elite academic institution.

None of this is news to people familiar with top elite academic institutions. But many young people from a low-income minority community may be the first member of their family to go to college. When such a person is being congratulated for having been accepted into some big-name college or university, they may not see the great risks there may be in this situation. Given the low academic standards in most public schools in low-income minority communities, the supposedly lucky student may have been getting top grades with ease in high school, and can be heading for a nasty shock when confronted with a wholly different situation at the college level.

What is at issue is not whether the student is qualified to be in college, but whether that student's particular qualifications are a match or a mismatch with the qualifications of the other students at the particular college or university that grants admission. Empirical evidence suggests that this can be a crucial factor.

In the University of California system, under affirmative action admissions policies, the black and Hispanic students admitted to the top-ranked campus at Berkeley had SAT scores just slightly above the national average. But the white students admitted to UC Berkeley had SAT scores more than 200 points higher— and the Asian American students had SAT scores somewhat higher than the whites.[53]

In this setting, most black students failed to graduate— and, as the number of black students admitted increased during the 1980s, the number graduating actually decreased.[54]

California voters voted to put an end to affirmative action admissions in the University of California system. Despite dire predictions that there would be a drastic reduction in the number of minority students in the UC system, there was in fact very little change in the total number of minority students admitted to the system as a whole. But there was a radical redistribution of minority students among the different campuses across the state.

There was a drastic reduction in the number going to the two top-ranked campuses— UC Berkeley and UCLA. Minority students were now going to those particular UC campuses where the other students had academic backgrounds more similar to their own, as measured by admissions test scores. Under these new conditions, the number of black and Hispanic students *graduating* from the University of California system as a whole *rose* by more than a thousand students over a four-year span.[55] There was also an increase of 63 percent in the number graduating in four years with a grade point average of 3.5 or higher.[56]

The minority students who fail to graduate under affirmative action admissions policies are by no means the only ones who are harmed by being admitted to institutions geared to students with better pre-college educational backgrounds. Many minority students who enter college expecting to major in challenging fields like science, technology, engineering or mathematics— called STEM fields— are forced to abandon such tough subjects and concentrate in easier fields. After affirmative action in admissions was banned in the University of California system, not only did more minority students graduate, the number graduating with degrees in the STEM fields rose by 51 percent.[57]

What is crucial from the standpoint of minority students being able to survive and flourish academically is not the absolute level of their pre-college educational qualifications, as measured by admissions test scores, but the *difference* between their test scores and the test scores of the other students at the particular institutions they attend. Minority students who score well above the average of American students as a whole on college admissions tests can nevertheless be turned into failures by being admitted to institutions where the other students score *even farther* above the average of American students as a whole.

Data from the Massachusetts Institute of Technology illustrate this situation. Data from MIT showed the black students there had average SAT math scores at the 90th percentile. But, although these students were in the top ten percent of American students in mathematics, they were in the *bottom* 10 percent of students at MIT, whose students' math scores were at the 99th percentile. The outcome was that 24 percent of these extremely well-qualified black students failed to graduate at MIT, and those who did graduate were concentrated in the lower half of their class.[58] In most American academic institutions, these same black students would have been among the best students on campus.

Some people might say that even those students who were concentrated in the lower half of their class at MIT gained the advantage of having been educated at one of the leading engineering schools in the world. But this is implicitly assuming that students automatically get a better education at a higher-ranked institution. However, we cannot dismiss the possibility that these students may learn *less* where the pace and complexity of the education is geared to students with an extraordinarily stronger pre-college educational background.

To test this possibility, we can turn to some fields, such as medicine and the law, where there are independent tests of how much the students have learned, after they have completed their formal education. The graduates of both medical schools and law schools cannot become licensed to practice their professions without passing these independent tests.

A study of five state-run medical schools found that the black-white difference in passing the U.S. Medical Licensing Examination was correlated with the black-white difference on the Medical College Admission Test before entering medical school.

In other words, blacks trained at medical schools where there was little difference between black and white students— in their scores on the test that got them admitted to medical school— had less difference between the races in their rates of passing the Medical Licensing test years later, after graduating from medical school.[59] The success or failure of blacks on these tests after graduation was correlated more with whether they were trained with other students whose admissions test scores were similar to theirs, rather than being correlated with whether the medical school was highly ranked or lower ranked.

Apparently they learned better where they were *not* mismatched by affirmative action admissions policies.

There were similar results in a comparison of law school graduates who took the independent bar examination, in order to become licensed as lawyers. George Mason University law school's student body as a whole had higher law school admissions test scores than the admissions test scores of the student body at the Howard University law school, a predominantly black institution. But the black students at both institutions had law school admissions test scores similar to each other. The net result was that black students entered the law school at George Mason University with admissions test scores lower than that of the other law school students there. But apparently not so at Howard University.

Data on the percentage of black students admitted to each law school who both graduated from law school and passed the bar examination on the first try showed that 30 percent of the black students at George Mason University law school did so— compared to 57 percent of the black students from the Howard University law school who did so.[60] Again, the students who were mismatched did not succeed as well as those who were not. As with the other examples, the students who were not mismatched seemed to learn better when taught in classes where the other students had educational preparation similar to their own.

These few examples need not be considered definitive. But they provide data that many other institutions refuse to release. When UCLA Professor Richard H. Sander sought to get California bar examination data, in order to test whether affirmative action admissions policies produced more black lawyers or *fewer* black lawyers, a lawsuit was threatened if the California Bar Association released that data.[61] The data were not released. Nor is this an unusual pattern. Academic institutions across the country, that proclaim the benefits of affirmative action "diversity," refuse to release data that would put such claims to the test.[62]

A study that declared affirmative action admissions policies a success— *The Shape of the River* by William Bowen and Derek Bok— was widely praised in the media, but its authors refused to let critics see the raw data from which they reached conclusions very different from the conclusions of other studies— based on data these other authors made available.[63] Moreover, other academic scholars found much to question about the conclusions reached by former university presidents Bowen and Bok.[64]

Where damaging information about the actual consequences of affirmative action admissions policies are brought to light and create a scandal, the response has seldom been to address the issue, but instead to denounce the person who revealed the scandalous facts as a "racist." This was the response when Professor Bernard Davis of the Harvard medical school said in the *New England Journal of Medicine* that black students there, and at other medical schools, were being granted diplomas "on a charitable basis." He called it "cruel" to admit students unlikely to meet medical school standards, and even more cruel "to abandon those standards and allow the trusting patients to pay for our irresponsibility."[65]

Although Professor Davis was denounced as a "racist," black economist Walter E. Williams had learned of such things elsewhere,[66] and there was a private communication from an official at the Harvard medical school some years earlier that such things were being proposed.[67]

Similarly, when a student at Georgetown University revealed data showing that the median score at which black students were admitted to that law school was lower than the test score at which any white student was admitted, the response was to denounce him as a "racist," rather than concentrating on the serious issue raised by that revelation.[68] That median score, incidentally, was at the 70th percentile, so these were not "unqualified" students, but students who would probably have more chance of success at some other law schools, and when later confronting the need to pass a bar exam to become lawyers.

Being a failure at an elite institution does a student no good. But the tenacity with which academic institutions fiercely resist anything that might force them to abandon counterproductive admissions practices suggests that these practices may be doing somebody some good. Even after California voters voted to end affirmative action admissions practices in the University of California system, that led to continuing efforts to circumvent this prohibition.[69] Why? What good does having a visible minority student presence on campus do, if most of them do not graduate?

One clue might be what many colleges have long done with their athletic teams in basketball and football, which can bring in millions of dollars in what are classified as "amateur" sports. Some successful college football coaches have incomes higher than the incomes of their college or university presidents. But the athletes on their teams have been paid nothing[70] for spending years providing entertainment for others, at the risk of bodily injuries— and the perhaps greater and longer-lasting risk to their character, from spending years pretending to be getting an education, when many are only doing enough to maintain their eligibility to play. An extremely small percentage of college athletes in basketball and football go on to a career in professional sports.

A disproportionate number of college basketball and football stars are black[71]— and academic institutions have not hesitated to misuse them in these ways. So we need not question whether these academic institutions are morally capable of bringing minority youngsters on campus to serve the institution's own interests. Nor need we doubt academics' verbal talents for rationalization, whether trying to convince others or themselves.[72]

The factual question is simply whether there are institutional interests being served by having a visible demographic representation of minority students on campus, whether those students get an education and graduate or not. The hundreds of millions of dollars of federal money that comes into an academic institution annually can be put at risk if ethnic minorities are seriously "under-represented" among the students, since that raises the prospect of under-representation being equated with racial discrimination. And that issue can be a legal threat to vast amounts of government money.

Nor is this the only outside pressure on academic institutions to continue affirmative action admissions policies that are damaging to the very groups supposedly being favored. George Mason University's law school was threatened with losing its accreditation if it did not continue admitting minority students who did not have qualifications as high as other students, even though data showed that this was not in the minority students' own best interests.[73] The reigning social justice fallacy that statistical disparities in group representation mean racial discrimination has major impacts. Minority students on campus are like human shields used to protect institutional interests— and casualties among human shields can be very high.

Many social policies help some groups while harming other groups. Affirmative action in academia manages to inflict harm on both the students who were not granted admissions, despite their qualifications, and also many of those students who were admitted to institutions where they were more likely to fail, even when they were fully qualified to succeed in other institutions.

Economic self-interest is by no means the only factor leading some individuals and institutions to persist in demonstrably counterproductive affirmative action admissions policies. Ideological crusades are not readily abandoned by people who are paying no price for being wrong, and who could pay a heavy price— personally and socially— for breaking ranks under fire and forfeiting both a cherished vision and a cherished place among fellow elites. As with the genetic determinists and the "sex education" advocates, there have been very few people willing to acknowledge facts that contradict the prevailing narrative.

Even where there is good news about people that surrogate decision-makers are supposedly helping, it seldom gets much attention when the good results have been achieved independently of surrogate decision-makers. For example, the fact that most of the rise of blacks out of poverty occurred in the decades *before* the massive government social programs of the 1960s, before the proliferation of charismatic "leaders," and before widespread media attention, has seldom been mentioned in the prevailing social justice narrative.

Neither has there been much attention paid to the fact that homicide rates among non-white males in the 1940s (who were overwhelmingly black males in those years) went *down* by 18 percent in that decade, followed by a further decline of 22 percent in the 1950s. Then suddenly that reversed in the 1960s,[74] when criminal laws were weakened, amid heady catchwords like "root causes" and "rehabilitation."

Perhaps the most dramatic— and most consequential— contrast between the pre-1960s progress of blacks and negative trends in the post-1960s era was that the proportion of black children born to unmarried women *quadrupled* from just under 17 percent in 1940 to just over 68 percent at the end of the century.[75]

Intellectual elites, politicians, activists and "leaders"— who took credit for the black progress that supposedly all began in the 1960s— took no responsibility for painful retrogressions that demonstrably did begin in the 1960s.

Such patterns are not peculiar to blacks or to the United States. Group preference policies in other countries did little for people in poverty, just as affirmative action did little for black Americans in poverty. The benefits of preferential treatment in India, Malaysia and Sri Lanka, for example, tended to go principally to more fortunate people in low-income groups in these countries,[76] just as in the United States.[77]

IMPLICATIONS

Where, fundamentally, did the social justice vision go wrong? Certainly not in hoping for a better world than the world we see around us today, with so many people suffering needlessly, in a world with ample resources to have better outcomes. But the painful reality is that no human being has either the vast range of consequential knowledge, or the overwhelming power, required to make the social justice ideal become a reality. Some fortunate societies have seen enough favorable factors come together to create basic prosperity and common decency among free people. But that is not enough for many social justice crusaders.

Intellectual elites may imagine that they have all the consequential knowledge required to create the social justice world they seek, despite considerable evidence to the contrary. But, even if they were somehow able to handle the knowledge problem, there still remains the problem of having enough power to do all that would need to be done. That is not just a problem for intellectual elites. It is an even bigger problem— and danger— for the people who might give them that power.

The history of totalitarian dictatorships that arose in the twentieth century, and were responsible for the deaths of millions of their own people in peacetime, should be an urgent warning against putting too much power in the hands of any human beings. That some of these disastrous regimes were established with the help of many sincere and earnest people, seeking high ideals and a better life for the less fortunate, should be an especially relevant warning to people seeking social justice, in disregard of the dangers.

It is hard to think of any power exercised by human beings over other human beings that has not been abused. Yet we must have laws and governments, because anarchy is worse. But we cannot just keep surrendering more and more of our freedoms to politicians, bureaucrats and judges— who are what elected governments basically consist of— in exchange for plausible-sounding rhetoric that we do not bother to subject to the test of facts.

Among the many facts that need to be checked is the actual track record of crusading intellectual elites, seeking to influence public policies and shape national institutions, on a range of issues extending from social justice to foreign policies and military conflict.

As regards social justice issues in general, and the situation of the poor in particular, intellectual elites who have produced a wide variety of policies that claim to help the poor, have shown a great reluctance to put the actual consequences of those policies to any empirical test. Often they have been hostile to others who have put these policies to some empirical test. Where social justice advocates have had the power to do so, they have often blocked access to data sought by scholars who want to do empirical tests on the consequences of such policies as affirmative action academic admissions policies.

Perhaps most surprising of all, many social justice advocates have shown little or no interest in remarkable examples of progress by the poor— when that progress was not based on the kinds of policies promoted in the name of social justice. The striking progress made by black Americans in the decades *before* the 1960s has been widely ignored. So has the demonstrable *harm* suffered by black Americans *after* the social justice policies of the 1960s. These included a sharp reversal of the homicide rate decline and a quadrupling of the proportion of black children born to unmarried women. Government policies made fathers a negative factor for mothers seeking welfare benefits.

Social justice advocates who denounce elite New York City public high schools that require an entrance examination for admissions pay no attention to the fact that black student admissions to such schools were much higher in the past, *before* the elementary schools and middle schools in black communities were ruined by the kinds of policies favored by social justice advocates. Back in 1938, the proportion of black students who graduated from elite Stuyvesant High School was almost as high as the proportion of blacks in the New York City population.[78]

As late as 1971, there were more black students than Asian students at Stuyvesant.[79] As of 1979, blacks were 12.9 percent of the students at Stuyvesant, but that declined to 4.8 percent by 1995.[80] By 2012, blacks were just 1.2 percent of the students at Stuyvesant.[81] Over a span of 33 years, the proportion of black students at Stuyvesant High School *fell* to less than *one tenth* of what it had been before. Neither of the usual suspects— genetics or racism— can explain these developments in those years. Nor is there any evidence of soul-searching by social justice advocates for how their ideas might have played a role in all this.

On an international scale, and on issues besides education, those with the social justice vision often fail to show any serious interest in the progress of the less fortunate, when it happens in ways unrelated to the social justice agenda. The rate of socioeconomic progress of black Americans before the 1960s is a classic example. But there has been a similar lack of interest in the ways by which poverty-stricken Eastern European Jewish immigrants, living in slums, rose to prosperity, or how similarly poverty-stricken Japanese immigrants in Canada did the same. In both cases, their current prosperity has been dealt with rhetorically, by calling their achievements "privilege."[82]

There have been many examples of peoples and places around the world that lifted themselves out of poverty in the second half of the twentieth century. These would include Hong Kong,[83] Singapore,[84] and South Korea.[85] In the last quarter of the twentieth century, the huge nations of India[86] and China[87] had vast millions of poor people rise out of poverty. The common denominator in all these places was that their rise out of poverty began after government micro-managing of the economy was reduced. This was especially ironic in the case of China, with a communist government.

With social justice advocates supposedly concerned with the fate of the poor, it may seem strange that they seem to have paid remarkably little attention to places where the poor have risen out of poverty at a dramatic rate and on a massive scale. That at least raises the question whether the social justice advocates' priorities are the poor themselves or the social justice advocates' own vision of the world and their own role in that vision.

What are those of us who are not followers of the social justice vision and its agenda to do? At a minimum, we can turn our attention from rhetoric to the realities of life. As the great Supreme Court Justice Oliver Wendell Holmes said, "think things instead of words."[88] Today it is especially important to get facts, rather than catchwords. These include not only current facts, but also the vast array of facts about what others have done in the past— both the successes and the failures. As the distinguished British historian Paul Johnson said:

> The study of history is a powerful antidote to contemporary arrogance. It is humbling to discover how many of our glib assumptions, which seem to us novel and plausible, have been tested before, not once but many times and in innumerable guises; and discovered to be, at great human cost, wholly false.[89]

NOTES

EPIGRAPH

Alan Greenspan, *The Age of Turbulence: Adventures in a New World* (New York: Penguin Press, 2007), p. 95.

CHAPTER 1: "EQUAL CHANCES" FALLACIES

1. Jean-Jacques Rousseau, *A Discourse on Inequality*, translated by Maurice Cranston (London: Penguin Books, 1984), p. 57.

2. Sam McCaig, "Where in the World Do NHL Players Come From?" *Sports Illustrated* (online), October 14, 2018; Helene Elliott, "California Hockey Has Come So Far," *Los Angeles Times*, September 6, 2020, p. D6; The Economist, *Pocket World in Figures: 2022 Edition* (London: Profile Books, 2021), pp. 14, 214; Shawn Hubler, "California's Population Dips During Tumultuous 2020," *New York Times*, May 8, 2021, p. A17.

3. Charles Issawi, "The Transformation of the Economic Position of the *Millets* in the Nineteenth Century," *Christians and Jews in the Ottoman Empire: The Functioning of a Plural Society*, Vol. I: *The Central Lands*, edited by Benjamin Braude and Bernard Lewis (New York: Holmes and Meier, 1982), pp. 262–263.

4. Yuan-li Wu and Chun-hsi Wu, *Economic Development in Southeast Asia: The Chinese Dimension* (Stanford: Hoover Institution Press, 1980), p. 51.

5. Jean Roche, *La Colonisation Allemande et le Rio Grande do Sul* (Paris: Institut Des Hautes Études de L'Amérique Latine, 1959), pp. 388–389.

6. R. Bayly Winder, "The Lebanese in West Africa," *Comparative Studies in Society and History*, Vol. IV, Issue 3 (April 1962), p. 309.

7. Jonathan I. Israel, *European Jewry in the Age of Mercantilism 1550–1750* (Oxford: Clarendon Press, 1985), p. 139.

8. Robert F. Foerster, *The Italian Emigration of Our Times* (New York: Arno Press, 1969), pp. 254–259, 261.

9. Haraprasad Chattopadhyaya, *Indians in Africa: A Socio-Economic Study* (Calcutta: Bookland Private Limited, 1970), p. 394.

10. Andrew Gibb, *Glasgow: The Making of a City* (London: Croom Helm, 1983), p. 116; Bruce Lenman, *An Economic History of Modern Scotland, 1660–1976* (London: B.T. Batsford, 1977), p. 180.

11. Amy Chua, *World on Fire: How Exporting Free Market Democracy Breeds Ethnic Hatred and Global Instability* (New York: Doubleday, 2003), p. 108.

12. Myron Weiner, *Sons of the Soil: Migration and Ethnic Conflict in India* (Princeton: Princeton University Press, 1978), pp. 102–104.

13. See, for example, Andrew D. Mellinger, Jeffrey D. Sachs, and John L. Gallup, "Climate, Coastal Proximity, and Development," *The Oxford Handbook of Economic Geography*, edited by Gordon L. Clark, Maryann P. Feldman, and Meric S. Gertler (Oxford: Oxford University Press, 2000); Ellen Churchill Semple, *Influences of Geographic Environment* (New York: Henry Holt and Company, 1911); Thomas Sowell, *Wealth, Poverty and Politics*, revised and enlarged edition (New York: Basic Books, 2016), 3–5, 8–10, 13–83.

14. Caryn E. Neumann, "Beer," *Germany and the Americas: Culture, Politics, and History*, edited by Thomas Adam (Santa Barbara, California: ABC-CLIO, 2005), Volume I, pp. 130–133.

15. Jim Mann, "Tsingtao Beer: Bottling Profits for China," *Los Angeles Times*, October 12, 1986, pp. F1, F7.

16. Robert F. Foerster, *The Italian Emigration of Our Times*, p. 261.

17. "Brazilian Beverage Market Is Evolving," *Brazilian Bulletin*, January 1975, p. 6.

18. Jürgen Tampke, *The Germans in Australia* (New York: Cambridge University Press, 2006), p. 101.

19. Marc Helmond, *Total Revenue Management (TRM): Case Studies, Best Practices and Industry Insights* (Cham, Switzerland: Springer, 2020), p. 167.

20. Horst Dornbusch, "Bavaria," *The Oxford Companion to Beer*, edited by Garrett Oliver (New York: Oxford University Press, 2012), p. 104.

21. Ulrich Bonnell Phillips, *The Slave Economy of the Old South: Selected Essays in Economic and Social History* (Baton Rouge: Louisiana State University Press, 1968), p. 269.

22. See, for example, Thomas Sowell, *Migrations and Cultures: A World View* (New York: Basic Books, 1996), pp. 2, 150, 153, 158, 164, 166, 176, 192, 207, 211, 218–219, 284–285, 289–290, 307, 312, 345, 353, 367.

23. For documented examples, see Thomas Sowell, *Wealth, Poverty and Politics*, revised and enlarged edition, pp. 396–402.

24. "Degrees Conferred, by Level, Discipline, and Gender, 2018–19," *Chronicle of Higher Education* (Almanac 2021–2022), August 20, 2021, p. 43.

25. Ibid.

26. See Diana Furchtgott-Roth, *Women's Figures: An Illustrated Guide to the Economic Progress of Women In America*, 2012 edition (Washington: AEI Press, 2012). See also Thomas Sowell, *Economic Facts and Fallacies*, second edition (New York: Basic Books, 2015), Chapter 3 and Thomas Sowell, *Affirmative Action Reconsidered: Was It Necessary in Academia?* (Washington: AEI Press, 1975), pp. 23–27.

27. Jessica Semega, Melissa Kollar, Emily A. Shrider, and John F. Creamer, "Income and Poverty in the United States: 2019," *Current Population Reports*, P60–270 (RV) (Washington: U.S. Government Printing Office, 2020 and 2021), pp. 11, 51.

28. Bureau of Labor Statistics, "Who Chooses Part-Time Work and Why?" *Monthly Labor Review*, March 2018, pp. 5–7. See also Thomas Sowell, *Economic Facts and Fallacies*, second edition, pp. 61, 69, 72, 74, 82–83, 89 and Thomas Sowell, *Affirmative Action Reconsidered*, pp. 23, 24. See also Diana Furchtgott-Roth, *Women's Figures*, 2012 edition, pp. 17–18.

29. See John Iceland and Ilana Redstone, "The Declining Earnings Gap between Young Women and Men in the United States, 1979–2018," *Social Science Research*, Vol. 92 (November 2020), pp. 1–11; Diana Furchtgott-Roth, *Women's Figures*, 2012 edition, pp. 14, 15, 16, 19; Thomas Sowell, *Affirmative Action Reconsidered*, pp. 28, 31, 32, 33; Warren Farrell, *Why Men Earn More: The Startling Truth Behind the Pay Gap and What Women Can Do About It* (New York: Amacom, 2005), p. xxiii; Anita U. Hattiangadi and Amy M. Habib, *A Closer Look at Comparable Worth*, second edition (Washington: Employment Policy Foundation, 2000), p. 43; Thomas Sowell, *Education: Assumptions versus History* (Stanford: Hoover Institution Press, 1986), pp. 95, 97; Laurence C. Baker, "Differences in Earnings Between Male and Female Physicians," *The New England Journal of Medicine*, April 11, 1996, p. 960; Marianne Bertrand and Kevin Hallock, "The Gender Gap in Top Corporate Jobs," *Industrial and Labor Relations Review*, October 2001, p. 17.

30. "The Economic Role of Women," *The Economic Report of the President, 1973* (Washington, D.C.: U.S. Government Printing Office, 1973), p. 105.

31. Sam Dean and Johana Bhuiyan, "Why are Black and Latino people still kept out of tech industry?" *San Francisco Chronicle*, July 7, 2020, p. C1.

32. U.S. Department of Education, *Digest of Education Statistics 2019*, 55th edition (Washington: National Center of Education Statistics, 2021), p. 345.

33. Ibid., p. 351.

34. Mohamed Suffian bin Hashim, "Problems and Issues of Higher Education Development in Malaysia," *Development of Higher Education in Southeast Asia: Problems and Issues*, edited by Yip Yat Hoong (Singapore: Regional Institute of Higher Education and Development, 1973), Table 8, pp. 70–71.

35. Donald L. Horowitz, *Ethnic Groups in Conflict* (Berkeley: University of California Press, 1985), p. 677; Myron Weiner, "The Pursuit of Ethnic Equality Through Preferential Policies: A Comparative Public Policy Perspective," *From Independence to Statehood*, edited by Robert B. Goldmann and A. Jeyaratnam Wilson (London:

Frances Pinter, 1984), p. 64; Cynthia H. Enloe, *Police, Military and Ethnicity: Foundations of State Power* (New Brunswick: Transaction Books, 1980), p. 143.

36. Fernand Braudel, *A History of Civilizations*, translated by Richard Mayne (New York: The Penguin Press, 1994), p. 17.

37. James Oliphant, "Faith's Role In Picking a New Justice," *Los Angeles Times*, April 22, 2010, p. A11; Peter Baker, "Kagan Is Sworn In as the Fourth Woman, and 112th Justice, on the Supreme Court," *New York Times*, August 8, 2010, pp. 1, 13; Julie Zauzmer, "Back Home, Supreme Court Nominee Is Active in a Liberal Episcopalian Church," *Washington Post*, February 4, 2017, p. B2; Julie Hirschfeld Davis, "In Highlight for President, Gorsuch Is Sworn In as Court's 113th Justice," *New York Times*, April 11, 2017, p. A19. This was by no means the only statistical disparity among the Justices. For 11 consecutive years, every Justice of the Supreme Court had a law degree from one of just 3 Ivy League law schools— Harvard, Yale and Columbia. Peter Baker, "Kagan Is Sworn In as the Fourth Woman, and 112th Justice, on the Supreme Court," *New York Times*, August 8, 2010, pp. 1, 13; William Wan, "The High Court's Ivy League Problem," *Washington Post*, July 13, 2018, p. A4; Nicholas Fandos, "Barrett Sworn In to Supreme Court After 52–48 Vote," *New York Times*, October 27, 2020, p. A1.

38. Aleksandra Sandstrom, "Faith on the Hill: The Religious Composition of the 116th Congress," Pew Research Center, January 3, 2019, p. 3.

39. Thomas Sowell, "New Light on Black I.Q.," *New York Times*, March 27, 1977, Sunday magazine section, pp. 56–58, 60, 62; Thomas Sowell, *Intellectuals and Society*, revised and enlarged edition (New York: Basic Books, 2011), Chapter 17.

40. Ana Amélia Freitas-Vilela, et al., "Maternal Dietary Patterns During Pregnancy and Intelligence Quotients in the Offspring at 8 Years of Age: Findings from the ALSPAC Cohort," *Maternal & Child Nutrition*, Vol. 14, Issue 1 (January 2018), pp. 1–11; Ingrid B. Helland, et al., "Maternal Supplementation with Very-Long-Chain n-3 Fatty Acids During Pregnancy and Lactation Augments

Children's IQ at 4 Years of Age," *Pediatrics*, Vol. 111, No. 1 (January 2003), pp. e39–e44.

41. See, for example, Helene McNulty, et al., "Effect of Continued Folic Acid Supplementation beyond the First Trimester of Pregnancy on Cognitive Performance in the Child: A Follow-up Study from a Randomized Controlled Trial (FASSTT Offspring Trial)," *BMC Medicine*, Volume 17 (2019), pp. 1–11; Aoife Caffrey, et al., "Effects of Maternal Folic Acid Supplementation During the Second and Third Trimesters of Pregnancy on Neurocognitive Development in the Child: An 11-Year Follow-up from a Randomised Controlled Trial," *BMC Medicine*, Volume 19 (2021), pp. 1–13; Ann P. Streissguth, Helen M. Barr, and Paul D. Sampson, "Moderate Prenatal Alcohol Exposure: Effects on Child IQ and Learning Problems at Age 7 1/2 Years," *Alcoholism: Clinical and Experimental Research*, Volume 14, No. 5 (September/October 1990), pp. 662–669; Ernest L. Abel and Robert J. Sokol, "Incidence of Fetal Alcohol Syndrome and Economic Impact of FAS-Related Anomalies," *Drug and Alcohol Dependence*, Volume 19, Issue 1 (January 1987), pp. 51–70; Johann K. Eberhart and Scott E. Parnell, "The Genetics of Fetal Alcohol Spectrum Disorders," *Alcoholism: Clinical and Experimental Research*, Volume 40, Issue 6 (June 2016), pp. 1154–1165; Edward P. Riley, M. Alejandra Infante, and Kenneth R. Warren, "Fetal Alcohol Spectrum Disorders: An Overview," *Neuropsychology Review*, Volume 21, Issue 2 (June 2011), pp. 73–80.

42. Julia M. Rohrer, Boris Egloff, and Stefan C. Schmukle, "Examining the Effects of Birth Order on Personality," *Proceedings of the National Academy of Sciences*, Vol. 112, No. 46 (November 17, 2015), p. 14225; Lillian Belmont and Francis A. Marolla, "Birth Order, Family Size, and Intelligence," *Science*, Vol. 182, No. 4117 (December 14, 1973), p. 1098; Sandra E. Black, Paul J. Devereux and Kjell G. Salvanes, "Older and Wiser? Birth Order and IQ of Young Men," *CESifo Economic Studies*, Vol. 57, 1/2011, pp. 109, 112, 116.

43. Alison L. Booth and Hiau Joo Kee, "Birth Order Matters: The Effect of Family Size and Birth Order on Educational Attainment," *Journal of Population Economics*, Vol. 22, No. 2 (April 2009), p. 377.

44. Philip S. Very and Richard W. Prull, "Birth Order, Personality Development, and the Choice of Law as a Profession," *Journal of Genetic Psychology*, Vol. 116, No. 2 (June 1, 1970), pp. 219–221; Richard L. Zweigenhaft, "Birth Order, Approval-Seeking and Membership in Congress," *Journal of Individual Psychology*, Vol. 31, No. 2 (November 1975), p. 208; William D. Altus, "Birth Order and Its Sequelae," *Science*, Vol. 151 (January 7, 1966), pp. 44–49.

45. William D. Altus, "Birth Order and Its Sequelae," *Science*, Vol. 151 (January 7, 1966), p. 45.

46. Jere R. Behrman and Paul Taubman, "Birth Order, Schooling, and Earnings," *Journal of Labor Economics*, Vol. 4, No. 3, Part 2: The Family and the Distribution of Economic Rewards (July 1986), p. S136; *Astronauts and Cosmonauts: Biographical and Statistical Data*, Revised August 31, 1993, Report Prepared by the Congressional Research Service, Library of Congress, Transmitted to the Committee on Science, Space, and Technology, U.S. House of Representatives, One Hundred Third Congress, Second Session, March 1994 (Washington: U.S. Government Printing Office, 1994), p. 19; Daniel S.P. Schubert, Mazie E. Wagner, and Herman J.P. Schubert, "Family Constellation and Creativity: Firstborn Predominance Among Classical Music Composers," *The Journal of Psychology*, Vol. 95, No. 1 (1977), pp. 147–149; Robert J. Gary-Bobo, Ana Prieto and Natalie Picard, "Birth Order and Sibship Sex Composition as Instruments in the Study of Education and Earnings," Discussion Paper No. 5514 (February 2006), Centre for Economic Policy Research, London, p. 22.

47. Amy L. Anderson, "Individual and Contextual Influences on Delinquency: The Role of the Single-Parent Family," *Journal of Criminal Justice*, Volume 30 (2002), pp. 575–587; Kathleen M. Ziol-Guest, Greg J. Duncan, and Ariel Kalil, "One-Parent Students Leave School Earlier," *Education Next*, Spring 2015, pp. 37–41; Nick Spencer, "Does Material Disadvantage Explain the Increased Risk of Adverse Health, Educational, and Behavioural Outcomes Among Children in Lone Parent Households in Britain? A Cross Sectional Study," *Journal of Epidemiology and Community Health*, Volume 59 (2005), pp. 152–157; James Bartholomew, *The Welfare State We're In* (London: Politico's, 2006), revised edition, pp. 275, 276, 278.

48. Maggie Gallagher, "Fatherless Boys Grow Up Into Dangerous Men," *Wall Street Journal*, December 1, 1998, p. A22; Dewey G. Cornell, Elissa P. Benedek, and David M. Benedek, "Characteristics of Adolescents Charged with Homicide: Review of 72 Cases," *Behavioral Sciences & the Law*, Vol. 5, No. 1 (1987), pp. 13, 14; Stephen Baskerville, "Is There Really a Fatherhood Crisis?" *The Independent Review*, Volume 8, No. 4 (Spring 2004), pp. 485–486; Delphine Theobald, David P. Farrington, and Alex Piquero, "Childhood Broken Homes and Adult Violence: An Analysis of Moderators and Mediators," *Journal of Criminal Justice*, Volume 41 (2013), pp. 44–45, 47–50.

49. Stephen Baskerville, "Is There Really a Fatherhood Crisis?" *The Independent Review*, Volume 8, No. 4 (Spring 2004), p. 485.

50. "Boys with Absentee Dads Twice as Likely to be Jailed," *Washington Post*, August 21, 1998, p. A3.

51. Bruce J. Ellis, John E. Bates, Kenneth A. Dodge, David M. Fergusson, L. John Horwood, Gregory S. Pettit, and Lianne Woodward, "Does Father Absence Place Daughters at Special Risk for Early Sexual Activity and Teenage Pregnancy?" *Child Development*, Vol. 74, No. 3 (May-June 2003), pp. 801–821; Stephen Baskerville, "Is There Really a Fatherhood Crisis?" *The Independent Review*, Volume 8, No. 4 (Spring 2004), p. 485; James Bartholomew, *The Welfare State We're In*, revised edition, p. 276.

52. See, for example, Theodore Dalrymple, *Life at the Bottom: The Worldview That Makes the Underclass* (Chicago: Ivan R. Dee, 2001), p. viii; James Bartholomew, *The Welfare State We're In*, revised edition, pp. 275, 276, 278.

53. See, for example, Theodore Dalrymple, *Life at the Bottom*; James Bartholomew, *The Welfare State We're In*, revised edition, Chapters 4 and 6.

54. "Choose Your Parents Wisely," *The Economist*, July 26, 2014, p. 22; Betty Hart and Todd R. Risley, *Meaningful Differences in the Everyday Experience of Young American Children* (Baltimore: Paul H. Brookes Publishing Co., 1995), pp. 123–124, 125–126, 128, 198–199, 247.

55. U.S. Bureau of the Census, "Selected Population Profile in the United States," *2019 American Community Survey*, 1-Year Estimates, Table S0201.

56. U.S. Bureau of the Census, "Age— All People (Both Sexes Combined) by Median and Mean Income: 1974 to 2020," *Current Population Survey, 1975–2021,* Annual Social and Economic Supplements (CPS ASEC), Table P–10.

57. The Economist, *Pocket World in Figures: 2022 Edition*, p. 18.

58. Roy E. H. Mellor and E. Alistair Smith, *Europe: A Geographical Survey of the Continent* (New York: Columbia University Press, 1979), p. 3; Antony R. Orme, "Coastal Environments," *The Physical Geography of Africa*, edited by William M. Adams, Andrew S. Goudie, and Antony R. Orme (Oxford: Oxford University Press, 1996), p. 238; Encyclopaedia Britannica, *Britannica Concise Encyclopedia*, revised and expanded edition (Chicago: Encyclopaedia Britannica, 2006), p. 643.

59. Roy E. H. Mellor and E. Alistair Smith, *Europe*, p. 3.

60. Ibid.

61. Adam Smith, *An Inquiry Into the Nature and Causes of the Wealth of Nations* (New York: Modern Library, 1937), pp. 20–21.

62. Adam Smith, *The Theory of Moral Sentiments* (Indianapolis: Liberty Classics, 1976), p. 337.

63. See, for example, William A. Hance, *The Geography of Modern Africa* (New York: Columbia University Press, 1964), pp. 3–6, 12–19, 32–33; Fernand Braudel, *A History of Civilizations*, translated by Richard Mayne, pp. 117–126; David E. Bloom, Jeffrey D. Sachs, Paul Collier, and Christopher Udry, "Geography, Demography, and Economic Growth in Africa," *Brookings Papers on Economic Activity*, Vol. 1998, No. 2 (1998), pp. 207–273. See also Thomas Sowell, *Conquests and Cultures: An International History* (New York: Basic Books, 1998), pp. 99–109.

64. Fernand Braudel, *A History of Civilizations*, translated by Richard Mayne, p. 120.

65. A.H.M. Jones, *The Later Roman Empire 284–602: A Social and Administrative Survey* (Norman: University of Oklahoma Press, 1964), Volume 2, pp. 841–842.

66. Ellen Churchill Semple, *The Geography of the Mediterranean Region: Its Relation to Ancient History* (New York: Henry Holt and Company, 1931), p. 5.

67. Ellen Churchill Semple, *Influences of Geographic Environment*, p. 280.

68. Ibid.

69. Andrew D. Mellinger, Jeffrey D. Sachs, and John L. Gallup, "Climate, Coastal Proximity, and Development," *The Oxford Handbook of Economic Geography*, edited by Gordon L. Clark, Maryann P. Feldman, and Meric S. Gertler, pp. 169, 177–179, 182. Note especially the world map on page 178.

70. See, for example, Frederick R. Troeh and Louis M. Thompson, *Soils and Soil Fertility*, sixth edition (Ames, Iowa: Blackwell, 2005), p. 330; Xiaobing Liu, et al., "Overview of Mollisols in the World: Distribution, Land Use and Management," *Canadian Journal of Soil Science*, Vol. 92 (2012), pp. 383–402; Darrell Hess, *McKnight's Physical Geography: A Landscape Appreciation*, eleventh edition (Upper Saddle River, New Jersey: Pearson Education, Inc., 2014), pp. 362–363.

71. Charles Murray, *Human Accomplishment: The Pursuit of Excellence in the Arts and Sciences, 800 B.C. to 1950* (New York: Harper Collins, 2003), pp. 355–361.

72. Andrew D. Mellinger, Jeffrey D. Sachs, and John L. Gallup, "Climate, Coastal Proximity, and Development," *The Oxford Handbook of Economic Geography*, edited by Gordon L. Clark, Maryann P. Feldman, and Meric S. Gertler, pp. 169, 180, 181.

73. Ibid., pp. 178, 179, 182, 183.

74. Robert J. Sharer, *The Ancient Maya*, fifth edition (Stanford: Stanford University Press, 1994), p. 455.

75. Jared Diamond, *Guns, Germs, and Steel: The Fates of Human Societies* (New York: W.W. Norton, 1997), p. 352.

76. David S. Landes, *The Wealth and Poverty of Nations: Why Some Are So Rich and Some So Poor* (New York: W.W. Norton & Company, 1998), pp. 4–5.

77. Ibid., p. 6.

78. See, for example, Paul Robert Magosci, *A History of Ukraine* (Seattle: University of Washington Press, 1996), p. 6; Tony Judt, *Postwar: A History of Europe Since 1945* (New York: Penguin Books, 2006), p. 648; Peter Duffy, "75 Years Later, Survivor Helps Commemorate Ukrainian Famine," *New York Times*, December 19, 2007, p. B3; Will Horner and Kirk Maltais, "Ukraine Tensions Drive Up Wheat Prices," *Wall Street Journal*, February 1, 2022, p. B11.

79. See, for example, Thomas Sowell, *Economic Facts and Fallacies*, second edition, Chapter 3. See also Diana Furchtgott-Roth, *Women's Figures*, 2012 edition.

80. "The World's Least Honest Cities," *The Telegraph.UK*, September 25, 2013.

81. Eric Felten, "Finders Keepers?" *Reader's Digest*, April 2001, pp. 102–107.

82. See Raymond Fisman and Edward Miguel, "Cultures of Corruption: Evidence from Diplomatic Parking Tickets," Working Paper 12312, National Bureau of Economic Research, June 2006, Table 1, pp. 19–22.

83. John Stuart Mill, *Collected Works of John Stuart Mill*, Vol. III: *Principles of Political Economy with Some of Their Applications to Social Philosophy*, edited by J.M. Robson (Toronto: University of Toronto Press, 1965), p. 882.

84. John P. McKay, *Pioneers for Profit: Foreign Entrepreneurship and Russian Industrialization 1885–1913* (Chicago: University of Chicago Press, 1970), pp. 176, 187; Linda M. Randall, *Reluctant Capitalists: Russia's Journey Through Market Transition* (New York: Routledge, 2001), pp. 56–57; Raghuram G. Rajan and

Luigi Zingales, *Saving Capitalism from the Capitalists* (Princeton: Princeton University Press, 2004), p. 57; Bryon MacWilliams, "Reports of Bribe-Taking at Russian Universities Have Increased, Authorities Say," *The Chronicle of Higher Education*, April 18, 2002 (online); Transparency International, *Transparency International Corruption Perceptions Index 2021* (Berlin: Transparency International Secretariat, 2022), pp. 2–3.

85. Karl Stumpp, *The German-Russians: Two Centuries of Pioneering* (Bonn: Edition Atlantic-Forum, 1967), p. 68.

86. Gurcharan Das, *India Unbound: The Social and Economic Revolution from Independence to the Global Information Age* (New York: Alfred A. Knopf, 2001), p. 143. For information on the overseas Chinese merchants, see Clifton A. Barton, "Trust and Credit: Some Observations Regarding Business Strategies of Ethnic Chinese Traders in South Vietnam," and Janet T. Landa, "The Political Economy of the Ethnically Homogenous Chinese Middleman Group in Southeast Asia: Ethnicity and Entrepreneurship in a Plural Society," in *The Chinese in Southeast Asia*, Volume 1: *Ethnicity and Economic Activity*, edited by Linda Y.C. Lim and L.A. Peter Gosling (Singapore: Mazuren Asia, 1983), pp. 53, 90.

87. Renée Rose Shield, *Diamond Stories: Enduring Change on 47th Street* (Ithaca, New York: Cornell University Press, 2002), Chapter 5.

88. Eric J. Evans, *The Shaping of Modern Britain: Identity, Industry and Empire, 1780–1914* (New York: Longman, 2011), p. 136.

89. Brian Murdoch, "Introduction," *German Literature of the Early Middle Ages*, edited by Brian Murdoch (Rochester, New York: Camden House, 2004), Volume 2, p. 10; Samantha Zacher, "Introduction to Medieval Literature," *A Companion to British Literature*, Volume I: *Medieval Literature 700–1450*, edited by Robert DeMaria, Jr., Heesok Chang, and Samantha Zacher (West Sussex, United Kingdom: Wiley-Blackwell, 2014), p. xxxv; Jean W. Sedlar, *East Central Europe in the Middle Ages, 1000–1500* (Seattle: University of Washington Press, 1994), pp. 440, 447, 449.

90. Gordon East, "The Concept and Political Status of the Shatter Zone," *Geographical Essays on Eastern Europe*, edited by Norman J.G. Pounds (Bloomington: Indiana University Press, 1961), p. 14.

91. Steven Pinker, *The Better Angels of Our Nature: Why Violence Has Declined* (New York: Viking, 2011), pp. 85–87.

92. David S. Landes, *The Wealth and Poverty of Nations*, p. 250.

93. Carlo M. Cipolla, *Literacy and Development in the West* (Baltimore: Penguin Books, 1969), pp. 16, 17.

94. See, for example, N.J.G. Pounds, *An Historical Geography of Europe* (Cambridge: Cambridge University Press, 1990); Charles Murray, *Human Accomplishment*, pp. 295–303.

95. Bernard Nkemdirim, "Social Change and the Genesis of Political Conflict in Nigeria," *Civilisations*, Vol. 25, Nos. 1–2 (1975), p. 94.

96. Thomas Sowell, *Affirmative Action Around the World: An Empirical Study* (New Haven: Yale University Press, 2004), p. 100; Amy Chua, *World on Fire*, pp. 108, 109.

97. Charles O. Hucker, *China's Imperial Past: An Introduction to Chinese History and Culture* (Stanford: Stanford University Press, 1975), p. 65; Jacques Gernet, *A History of Chinese Civilization*, translated by J.R. Foster (New York: Cambridge University Press, 1985), pp. 69, 138, 140.

98. Jacques Gernet, *A History of Chinese Civilization*, translated by J.R. Foster, pp. 288, 333–336.

CHAPTER 2: RACIAL FALLACIES

1. Madison Grant, *The Passing of the Great Race or the Racial Basis of European History*, revised edition (New York: Charles Scribner's Sons, 1918), p. 100.

2. U.S. Bureau of the Census, "The Social and Economic Status of the Black Population in the United States: An Historical View, 1790–1978," *Current Population Reports*, Series P-23, No. 80 (Washington: Bureau of the Census, no date), p. 31; U.S. Bureau of the Census, "Race and Hispanic Origin of Householder— Families

by Median and Mean Income: 1947 to 2021," *Current Population Survey, 1948–2022*, Annual Social and Economic Supplements (CPS ASEC), Table F–5.

3. U.S. Bureau of the Census, "Selected Population Profile in the United States," *2019 American Community Survey*, 1-Year Estimates, Table S0201.

4. Ibid.

5. Ibid.

6. Ibid.

7. U.S. Bureau of the Census, "Selected Characteristics of People 15 Years Old and Over by Total Money Income in 2020, Work Experience in 2020, Race, Hispanic Origin, and Sex," *Current Population Survey, 2021*, Annual Social and Economic Supplement (CPS ASEC), Table PINC–01.

8. A study by the Federal Reserve Bank of St. Louis found that 2 percent of black families were millionaires. (Ana Hernández Kent and Lowell R. Ricketts, "Wealth Gaps between White, Black and Hispanic Families in 2019," Federal Reserve Bank of St. Louis, January 5, 2021.) Census data show that there were more than ten million black families. This means that there were thousands of black millionaire families. U.S. Bureau of the Census, "Family Groups: 2020," *Current Population Survey, 2020*, Annual Social and Economic Supplement, Table FG10.

9. "A League of Their Own," *Forbes*, June/July 2022, p. 21; "Forbes 400," *Forbes*, October 2020, p. 104.

10. Emily A. Shrider, Melissa Kollar, Frances Chen and Jessica Semega, "Income and Poverty in the United States: 2020," *Current Population Reports*, P60–273 (Washington: U.S. Government Publishing Office, 2021), pp. 57–59.

11. U.S. Bureau of the Census, "Poverty Status of Families, by Type of Family, Presence of Related Children, Race, and Hispanic Origin: 1959 to 2020," *Current Population Survey, 1960–2021*, Annual Social and Economic Supplements (CPS ASEC), Table 4; Emily A. Shrider, Melissa Kollar, Frances Chen and Jessica

Semega, "Income and Poverty in the United States: 2020," *Current Population Reports*, P60–273, pp. 14, 56.

12. U.S. Bureau of the Census, "Poverty Status of Families, by Type of Family, Presence of Related Children, Race, and Hispanic Origin: 1959 to 2020," *Current Population Survey, 1960–2021*, Annual Social and Economic Supplements (CPS ASEC), Table 4.

13. Ibid.

14. These data from the New York State Education Department are cited in Thomas Sowell, *Charter Schools and Their Enemies* (New York: Basic Books, 2020), pp. 49, 140–187. Such data are available on the Internet for anyone who wants to compare charter school results with results in the same communities, whether for research purposes or for making choices of places to send their own children.

15. Data from the New York State Education Department are shown in Thomas Sowell, *Charter Schools and Their Enemies*, p. 49.

16. E. Franklin Frazier, "The Impact of Urban Civilization Upon Negro Family Life," *American Sociological Review*, Vol. 2, No. 5 (October 1937), p. 615.

17. Charles Lanman, *Dictionary of the United States Congress* (Washington: Government Printing Office, 1864), p. 537; Grady McWhiney, *Cracker Culture: Celtic Ways in the Old South* (Tuscaloosa: University of Alabama Press, 1988), p. 253.

18. Lewis Cecil Gray, *History of Agriculture in the Southern United States to 1860* (Washington: Carnegie Institution of Washington, 1933), Vol. II, p. 831.

19. Rupert B. Vance, *Human Geography of the South: A Study in Regional Resources and Human Adequacy* (Chapel Hill: University of North Carolina Press, 1932), pp. 167–168, 175.

20. Grady McWhiney, *Cracker Culture*, p. 196.

21. Alexis de Tocqueville, *Democracy in America* (New York: Alfred A. Knopf, 1989), Vol. I, pp. 362–363.

22. Frederick Law Olmsted, *The Cotton Kingdom: A Traveller's Observations on Cotton and Slavery in the American Slave States,*

edited by Arthur M. Schlesinger (New York: Alfred A. Knopf, 1953), pp. 12, 64, 65, 87, 90, 147, 327, 391.

23. Robert E. Lee, *Lee's Dispatches: Unpublished Letters of General Robert E. Lee, C.S.A. to Jefferson Davis and the War Department of the Confederate States of America, 1862–65*, edited by Douglas Southall Freeman, New Edition (New York: G.P. Putnam's Sons, 1957), p. 8.

24. Hinton Rowan Helper, *The Impending Crisis of the South: How to Meet It*, enlarged edition (New York: A. B. Burdick, 1860), pp. 40, 41, 44, 381.

25. Ulrich Bonnell Phillips, *The Slave Economy of the Old South: Selected Essays in Economic and Social History*, edited by Eugene D. Genovese (Baton Rouge: Louisiana State University Press, 1968), p. 107.

26. Rupert B. Vance, *Human Geography of the South*, pp. 148, 168, 304.

27. U.S. Bureau of the Census, "Total Population," *2011–2015 American Community Survey*, 5-Year Estimates, Table B01003; U.S. Bureau of the Census, "Median Household Income in the Past 12 Months (In 2015 Inflation-Adjusted Dollars)," *2011–2015 American Community Survey*, 5-Year Estimates, Table B19013.

28. Brett Barrouquere and Dylan T. Lovan, "Kentucky County Feels Food Stamp Reductions Sharply," *Washington Post*, February 2, 2014, p. A5.

29. See the data from the following publications: U.S. Bureau of the Census, *Per Capita Income, Median Family Income, and Low Income Status in 1969 for States, Standard Metropolitan Statistical Areas, and Counties: 1970* (Washington: U.S. Government Printing Office, 1974), pp. 7, 83; U.S. Bureau of the Census, *County and City Data Book, 1972* (Washington: U.S. Government Printing Office, 1973), pp. 19, 186, 189, 198, 201; U.S. Bureau of the Census, *County and City Data Book, 1983* (Washington: U.S. Government Printing Office, 1983), pp. 26, 214, 222, 228, 236; U.S. Bureau of the Census, *1980 Census of Population*, Volume 1: *General Social and Economic Characteristics*, Part 1, United States Summary, PC80-1–C1 (Washington: U.S. Government Printing Office, 1983),

p. 1–10t; U.S. Bureau of the Census, *County and City Data Book: 1994* (Washington: U.S. Government Printing Office, 1994), pp. 23, 214, 219, 228, 233; U.S. Bureau of the Census, *1990 Census of Population: Social and Economic Characteristics, United States,* 1990 CP–2–1 (Washington: U.S. Government Printing Office, 1993), p. 48; U.S. Bureau of the Census, *County and City Data Book: 2000* (Washington: U.S. Government Printing Office, 2001), pp. 33, 34, 81, 82, 210, 225, 226; U.S. Bureau of the Census, "Money Income in the United States: 1997 (With Separate Data on Valuation of Noncash Benefits)," *Current Population Reports,* P60–200 (Washington: U.S. Government Printing Office, 1998), p. vii; U.S. Bureau of the Census, *2020 Poverty and Median Household Income Estimates— Counties, States, and National,* Small Area Income and Poverty Estimates (SAIPE) Program, Release date: December 2021; U.S. Bureau of the Census, "QuickFacts" for Clay County, Kentucky and Owsley County, Kentucky, downloaded on January 12, 2023; Emily A. Shrider, Melissa Kollar, Frances Chen and Jessica Semega, "Income and Poverty in the United States: 2020," *Current Population Reports,* P60–273, p. 27.

30. Annie Lowrey, "Bluegrass-State Blues," *New York Times Magazine,* June 29, 2014, p. 13.

31. U.S. Bureau of the Census, "Selected Characteristics of the Total and Native Populations in the United States," *2010–2014 American Community Survey,* 5-Year Estimates, Table S0601.

32. See the data from the following publications: U.S. Bureau of the Census, *Per Capita Income, Median Family Income, and Low Income Status in 1969 for States, Standard Metropolitan Statistical Areas, and Counties: 1970,* pp. 7, 83; U.S. Bureau of the Census, *County and City Data Book, 1972,* pp. 19, 186, 189, 198, 201; U.S. Bureau of the Census, *County and City Data Book, 1983,* pp. 26, 214, 222, 228, 236; U.S. Bureau of the Census, *1980 Census of Population,* Volume 1: *General Social and Economic Characteristics,* Part 1, United States Summary, PC80–1–C1, p. 1–10t; U.S. Bureau of the Census, *County and City Data Book: 1994,* pp. 23, 214, 219, 228, 233; U.S. Bureau of the Census, *1990 Census of Population: Social and Economic Characteristics, United States,* 1990 CP–2–1, p. 48; U.S. Bureau of the Census, *County and City Data Book: 2000,* pp. 33, 34, 81, 82, 210, 225, 226; U.S. Bureau of the Census, "Money Income in the

United States: 1997 (With Separate Data on Valuation of Noncash Benefits)," *Current Population Reports*, P60–200, p. vii; U.S. Bureau of the Census, *2020 Poverty and Median Household Income Estimates— Counties, States, and National*, Small Area Income and Poverty Estimates (SAIPE) Program, Release date: December 2021; U.S. Bureau of the Census, "QuickFacts" for the following counties in Kentucky: Breathitt, Clay, Jackson, Lee, Leslie, and Mogoffin, downloaded on November 15, 2022; Emily A. Shrider, Melissa Kollar, Frances Chen and Jessica Semega, "Income and Poverty in the United States: 2020," *Current Population Reports*, P60–273, p. 27.

33. Ellen Churchill Semple, *Influences of Geographic Environment* (New York: Henry Holt and Company, 1911), p. 113.

34. Ibid.

35. See, for example, J.R. McNeill, *The Mountains of the Mediterranean World: An Environmental History* (New York: Cambridge University Press, 1992), pp. 27, 44, 46, 104, 110, 142–143; Ellen Churchill Semple, *Influences of Geographic Environment*, pp. 521, 522, 530, 531, 599, 600; Fernand Braudel, *The Mediterranean and the Mediterranean World in the Age of Philip II*, translated by Siân Reynolds (Berkeley: University of California Press, 1995), Vol. I, pp. 38, 46, 57, 97; Rupert B. Vance, *Human Geography of the South*, pp. 242, 246–247; Edward C. Banfield, *The Moral Basis of a Backward Society* (New York: The Free Press, 1958). See also James N. Gregory, *The Southern Diaspora: How The Great Migrations of Black and White Southerners Transformed America* (Chapel Hill: University of North Carolina Press, 2005), p. 76. A revealing elaboration of the American hillbilly culture was part of a best-selling book by J.D. Vance, *Hillbilly Elegy: A Memoir of a Family and Culture in Crisis* (New York: HarperCollins, 2016).

36. Barack Obama, *Dreams from My Father: A Story of Race and Inheritance* (New York: Crown Publishers, 2004), p. 254.

37. J. Todd Moye, *Freedom Flyers: The Tuskegee Airmen of World War II* (New York: Oxford University Press, 2010), especially p. 13; Martin Weil, "Benjamin O. Davis, Jr., 89, Dies; First Black General in Air Force," *Washington Post*, July 6, 2002, p. B7; "Black

Colonel Getting General's Rank," *New York Times*, January 26, 1970, p. 13; Nick Thimmesch, "'Chappie' James: A Remarkable Human Being," *Human Events*, March 18, 1978, p. 218.

38. Alexis de Tocqueville, *Democracy in America*, Vol. I, p. 365.

39. Frederick Law Olmsted, *The Cotton Kingdom*, edited by Arthur M. Schlesinger, pp. 476n, 614–622.

40. Hinton Rowan Helper, *The Impending Crisis of the South*, enlarged edition, p. 34.

41. Grady McWhiney, *Cracker Culture*, Chapters 2 and 3; David Hackett Fischer, *Albion's Seed: Four British Folkways in America* (New York: Oxford University Press, 1989), pp. 365–368, 740–743.

42. [Daniel Patrick Moynihan], *The Negro Family: The Case for National Action* (Washington: Government Printing Office, 1965), p. 8. Moynihan was not identified as the author, when this was issued as an anonymous government publication. Only after it became controversial was Moynihan identified as the author.

43. See, for example, the data in Charles Murray, *Coming Apart: The State of White America 1960–2010* (New York: Crown Forum, 2012), p. 160.

44. Ibid.

45. Ibid.; [Daniel Patrick Moynihan], *The Negro Family*, p. 8.

46. Centers for Disease Control and Prevention, U.S. Department of Health and Human Services, "Births: Final Data for 2000," *National Vital Statistics Reports*, Vol. 50, No. 5 (February 12, 2002), Table 19, p. 49.

47. Charles Murray, *Coming Apart*, p. 161.

48. James Bartholomew, *The Welfare of Nations* (Washington: The Cato Institute, 2016), p. 164.

49. Oliver Wendell Holmes, *Collected Legal Papers* (New York: Peter Smith, 1952), pp. 230–231.

50. John Dewey, for example, said of people who disagreed with him over whether the disarmament treaties he favored were as effective in deterring war as a military defense build-up would be that they had "the stupidity of habit-bound minds." John Dewey, "Outlawing Peace by Discussing War," *New Republic*, May 16, 1928, p. 370. Another prominent early Progressive, Professor Edward A. Ross, author of 28 books, referred to people with different views as "kept" spokesmen for special interests, a "mercenary corps" as contrasted with "us champions of the social welfare." Edward Alsworth Ross, *Seventy Years of It: An Autobiography* (New York: D. Appleton-Century Company, 1936), pp. 97–98. Among later Progressives, Professor Paul Krugman, in his book *Arguing with Zombies* referred to the "dishonesty," "bad faith" and "zombie" ideas of conservatives. Paul Krugman, *Arguing With Zombies: Economics, Politics and the Fight For a Better Future* (New York: W.W. Norton, 2021), pp. 7–8. In a similar vein, Professor Andrew Hacker simply declared that "conservatives don't really care whether black Americans are happy or unhappy." Andrew Hacker, *Two Nations: Black and White, Separate, Hostile, Unequal* (New York: Charles Scribner's Sons, 1992), p. 51.

51. Madison Grant, a central figure among the early Progressives, said: "There exists to-day a widespread and fatuous belief in the power of environment, as well as of education and opportunity to alter heredity, which arises from the dogma of the brotherhood of man, derived in its turn from the loose thinkers of the French Revolution and their American mimics." Madison Grant, *The Passing of the Great Race or the Racial Basis of European History*, revised edition, p. 16. See also Carl Brigham, *A Study of American Intelligence* (Princeton: Princeton University Press, 1923), pp. xx, xxi, 75–78, 143–147, 154, 189, 190–192, 194, 197, 202, 209–210. See also "Foreword," by Robert M. Yerkes on pages vii–viii; Clarence S. Yoakum and Robert M. Yerkes, *Army Mental Tests* (New York: Henry Holt and Company, 1920), pp. 17, 30; [Robert M. Yerkes,] National Academy of Sciences, *Psychological Examining in the United States Army* (Washington: Government Printing Office, 1921), Vol. XV, Part III, pp. 553, 742, 785, 789, 791.

52. Otto Klineberg, *Race Differences* (New York: Harper & Brothers, 1935), p. 182.

53. James M. McPherson, *The Abolitionist Legacy: From Reconstruction to the NAACP* (Princeton: Princeton University Press, 1975), pp. 165, 172–174.

54. Ibid., pp. 206, 367, 371–372; John Dittmer, *Black Georgia in the Progressive Era: 1900–1920* (Urbana: University of Illinois Press, 1977), p. 115. See also pp. 141–148. James D. Anderson, *The Education of Blacks in the South, 1860–1935* (Chapel Hill: University of North Carolina Press, 2010), pp. 4, 20–23, 94–102.

55. Jason L. Riley, "Philanthropy and Black Education," *City Journal,* Summer 2016, pp. 82, 84, 86.

56. John Dittmer, *Black Georgia in the Progressive Era,* p. 115.

57. Mandel Sherman and Cora B. Key, "The Intelligence of Isolated Mountain Children," *Child Development,* Vol. 3, No. 4 (December 1932), pp. 279, 283. See also Lester R. Wheeler, "A Comparative Study of the Intelligence of East Tennessee Mountain Children," *Journal of Educational Psychology,* Vol. XXXIII, No. 5 (May 1942), pp. 327–328; L.R. Wheeler, "The Intelligence of East Tennessee Mountain Children," *Journal of Educational Psychology,* Volume 23, Issue 5 (May 1932), pp. 361, 363.

58. Philip E. Vernon, *Intelligence and Cultural Environment* (London: Methuen & Co., Ltd., 1969), p. 155.

59. Hugh Gordon, *Mental and Scholastic Tests Among Retarded Children* (London: His Majesty's Stationery Office, 1923), p. 39.

60. Rudolf Pintner, *Intelligence Testing: Methods and Results* (New York: Henry Holt and Company, 1923), p. 352; Rudolph Pintner and Ruth Keller, "Intelligence Tests of Foreign Children," *Journal of Educational Psychology,* Volume 13, No. 4 (1922), pp. 214, 215.

61. Clifford Kirkpatrick, *Intelligence and Immigration* (Baltimore: The Williams & Wilkins Company, 1926), pp. 24, 31, 34.

62. Otto Klineberg, *Race Differences,* pp. 182–183.

63. U.S. Bureau of the Census, "Total Population," *2011–2015 American Community Survey,* 5-Year Estimates, Table B01003; U.S. Bureau of the Census, "Median Household Income in the

Past 12 Months (In 2015 Inflation-Adjusted Dollars)," *2011–2015 American Community Survey*, 5-Year Estimates, Table B19013; U.S. Bureau of the Census, *2020 Poverty and Median Household Income Estimates— Counties, States, and National*, Small Area Income and Poverty Estimates (SAIPE) Program, Release date: December 2021; U.S. Bureau of the Census, "QuickFacts" for the following counties in Kentucky: Breathitt, Clay, Jackson, Lee, Leslie, Mogoffin, and Owsley, downloaded on November 15, 2022 and January 12, 2023; Emily A. Shrider, Melissa Kollar, Frances Chen and Jessica Semega, "Income and Poverty in the United States: 2020," *Current Population Reports*, P60–273, p. 27. See also Brett Barrouquere and Dylan T. Lovan, "Kentucky County Feels Food Stamp Reductions Sharply," *Washington Post*, February 2, 2014, p. A5; Annie Lowrey, "Bluegrass-State Blues," *New York Times Magazine*, June 29, 2014, p. 13.

64. Mandel Sherman and Cora B. Key, "The Intelligence of Isolated Mountain Children," *Child Development*, Vol. 3, No. 4 (December 1932), pp. 279, 283.

65. Lester R. Wheeler, "A Comparative Study of the Intelligence of East Tennessee Mountain Children," *Journal of Educational Psychology*, Vol. XXXIII, No. 5 (May 1942), pp. 327, 328. See also L. R. Wheeler, "The Intelligence of East Tennessee Mountain Children," *Journal of Educational Psychology*, Volume 23, Issue 5 (May 1932), pp. 360, 363. "A study by Lacy, for example, showed that the average I.Q. of colored children dropped steadily from 99 to 87 in the first four school grades, whereas the White I.Q. remained almost stationary." Otto Klineberg, "Mental Testing of Racial and National Groups," *Scientific Aspects of the Race Problem*, edited by Herbert Spencer Jennings (Washington: Catholic University Press, 1941), p. 280.

66. Lester R. Wheeler, "A Comparative Study of the Intelligence of East Tennessee Mountain Children," *Journal of Educational Psychology*, Vol. XXXIII, No. 5 (May 1942), p. 322.

67. Ibid., pp. 327, 328.

68. Ellen Churchill Semple, *Influences of Geographic Environment*, p. 532.

69. See, for example, J.R. McNeill, *The Mountains of the Mediterranean World*, pp. 27, 44, 46, 104, 110, 142–143; Ellen Churchill Semple,

Influences of Geographic Environment, pp. 521, 522, 530, 531, 599, 600; Fernand Braudel, *The Mediterranean and the Mediterranean World in the Age of Philip II*, translated by Siân Reynolds, Vol. I, pp. 38, 46, 57, 97; Rupert B. Vance, *Human Geography of the South*, pp. 242, 246–247; Edward C. Banfield, *The Moral Basis of a Backward Society*; J.D. Vance, *Hillbilly Elegy*. See also James N. Gregory, *The Southern Diaspora*, p. 76.

70. Sandra Scarr and Richard A. Weinberg, "IQ Test Performance of Black Children Adopted by White Families," *American Psychologist* (October 1976), pp. 726–739.

71. Linda O. McMurry, *George Washington Carver: Scientist and Symbol* (New York: Oxford University Press, 1981), pp. 8–9, 12, 13–20.

72. Carl C. Brigham, *A Study of American Intelligence*, p. 190.

73. H.H. Goddard, "The Binet Tests in Relation to Immigration," *Journal of Psycho-Asthenics*, Vol. 18, No. 2 (December 1913), p. 110.

74. Jonathan Peter Spiro, *Defending the Master Race: Conservation, Eugenics, and the Legacy of Madison Grant* (Burlington: University of Vermont Press, 2009), p. 98.

75. Thomas C. Leonard, "Eugenics and Economics in the Progressive Era," *Journal of Economic Perspectives*, Vol. 19, No. 4 (Fall 2005), p. 211.

76. Jonathan Peter Spiro, *Defending the Master Race*, p. 99.

77. Edward Alsworth Ross, *The Old World in the New: The Significance of Past and Present Immigration to the American People* (New York: The Century Company, 1914), pp. 285–286.

78. Edward Alsworth Ross, "Who Outbreeds Whom?" *Proceedings of the Third Race Betterment Conference* (Battle Creek, Michigan: Race Betterment Foundation, 1928), p. 77.

79. John L. Gillin, "In Memoriam: Edward Alsworth Ross," *The Midwest Sociologist*, Vol. 14, No. 1 (Fall 1951), p. 18; Howard W. Odum, "Edward Alsworth Ross: 1866–1951," *Social Forces*, Vol. 30, No. 1 (October 1951), p. 126.

80. Edward Alsworth Ross, *Sin and Society: An Analysis of Latter-Day Iniquity* (Boston: Houghton-Mifflin Company, 1907), pp. ix–xi.

81. Julius Weinberg, *Edward Alsworth Ross and the Sociology of Progressivism* (Madison: The State Historical Society of Wisconsin, 1972), p. 136.

82. See, for example, Roscoe Pound, "The Theory of Judicial Decision. III. A Theory of Judicial Decision For Today," *Harvard Law Review*, Vol. 36, No. 8 (June 1923), pp. 940–959; Roscoe Pound, *Law and Morals* (Chapel Hill, North Carolina: The University of North Carolina Press, 1924); Roscoe Pound, *Criminal Justice in The American City—A Summary*, Part VII (Cleveland Foundation, 1922). See also Julius Weinberg, *Edward Alsworth Ross and the Sociology of Progressivism*, pp. 136–137. See also Walter K. Olson, *Schools for Misrule: Legal Academia and an Overlawyered America* (New York: Encounter Books, 2011), pp. 6, 40; Robert Heineman, *Authority and the Liberal Tradition: From Hobbes to Rorty* (New Brunswick, New Jersey: Transaction Publishers, 1994), second edition, pp. 129–131; James Davids, Erik Gustafson, and Sherena Arrington, *Clashing Worldviews in the U.S. Supreme Court: Rehnquist vs. Blackmun* (Lanham, Maryland: Lexington Books, 2020), pp. 41–42; David M. Rabban, *Law's History: American Legal Thought and the Transatlantic Turn to History* (New York: Cambridge University Press, 2013), pp. 423–471.

83. "Dr. R.T. Ely Dies; Noted Economist," *New York Times*, October 5, 1943, p. 25; See Thomas Sowell, *Intellectuals and Race* (New York: Basic Books, 2013), pp. 31, 33, 34–35.

84. Thomas Sowell, *Intellectuals and Race*, pp. 29, 30, 33, 34, 35; Lawrence J. Rhoades, *A History of the American Sociological Association: 1905–1980* (Washington: American Sociological Association, 1980), pp. 1, 2, 5; William E. Spellman, "The Economics of Edward Alsworth Ross," *American Journal of Economics and Sociology*, Vol. 38, No. 2 (April 1979), pp. 132–133.

85. Thomas Sowell, *Intellectuals and Race*, pp. 29, 30, 31, 33, 34, 35.

86. Ibid., pp. 29–35.

87. Michael S. Lawlor, *The Economics of Keynes in Historical Context: An Intellectual History of the General Theory* (New York: Palgrave Macmillan, 2006), p. 305n.

88. Thomas Sowell, *Intellectuals and Race,* pp. 24–43.

89. Carl N. Degler, *In Search of Human Nature: The Decline and Revival of Darwinism in American Social Thought* (New York: Oxford University Press, 1991), p. 43; Richard Overy, *The Twilight Years: The Paradox of Britain Between the Wars* (New York: Viking, 2009), pp. 104–105.

90. Thomas C. Leonard, "Eugenics and Economics in the Progressive Era," *Journal of Economic Perspectives,* Vol. 19, No. 4 (Fall 2005), p. 216.

91. "Obituary: Sir Francis Galton," *Journal of the Royal Statistical Society,* Vol. 74, No. 3 (February 1911), p. 315; Mark H. Haller, *Eugenics: Hereditarian Attitudes in American Thought* (New Brunswick: Rutgers University Press, 1963), p. 11.

92. Richard T. Ely, "The Price of Progress," *Administration,* Vol. III, No. 6 (June 1922), p. 662.

93. Thomas C. Leonard, "Eugenics and Economics in the Progressive Era," *Journal of Economic Perspectives,* Vol. 19, No. 4 (Fall 2005), p. 212.

94. Ibid., p. 213.

95. Ibid., p. 214.

96. Madison Grant, *The Passing of the Great Race or the Racial Basis of European History,* revised edition, p. xxi.

97. Ibid., p. 49.

98. Matthew Pratt Guterl, *The Color of Race in America: 1900–1940* (Cambridge, Massachusetts: Harvard University Press, 2001), p. 67.

99. Sidney Fine, "Richard T. Ely, Forerunner of Progressivism, 1880–1901," *Mississippi Valley Historical Review,* Vol. 37, No. 4 (March 1951), pp. 609, 610.

100. Dr. R.T. Ely Dies; Noted Economist," *New York Times*, October 5, 1943, p. 25; Sidney Fine, "Richard T. Ely, Forerunner of Progressivism, 1880–1901," *Mississippi Valley Historical Review*, Vol. 37, No. 4 (March 1951), pp. 613, 614.

101. Henry C. Taylor, "Richard Theodore Ely: April 13, 1854-October 4, 1943," *The Economic Journal*, Vol. 54, No. 213 (April 1944), p. 137.

102. Thomas C. Leonard, "Eugenics and Economics in the Progressive Era," *Journal of Economic Perspectives*, Vol. 19, No. 4 (Fall 2005), p. 215.

103. Henry C. Taylor, "Richard Theodore Ely: April 13, 1854-October 4, 1943," *The Economic Journal*, Vol. 54, No. 213 (April 1944), p. 133.

104. Jonah Goldberg, *Liberal Fascism: The Secret History of the American Left from Mussolini to the Politics of Meaning* (New York: Doubleday, 2007), p. 83.

105. Arthur S. Link, *Woodrow Wilson and the Progressive Era: 1910–1917* (New York: Harper & Brothers Publishers, 1954), pp. 64–66; Tom Lewis, *Washington: A History of Our National City* (New York: Basic Books, 2015), pp. 272–275.

106. Lloyd E. Ambrosius, *Woodrow Wilson and American Internationalism* (New York: Cambridge University Press, 2017), p. 80.

107. Larry Walker, "Woodrow Wilson, Progressive Reform, and Public Administration," *Political Science Quarterly*, Vol. 104, No. 3 (Autumn 1989), pp. 512–513; Ronald J. Pestritto, *Woodrow Wilson and the Roots of Modern Liberalism* (Lanham, Maryland: Rowman & Littlefield, 2005), pp. 255, 259, 260; Woodrow Wilson, *The State: Elements of Historical and Practical Politics*, revised edition (Boston: D.C. Heath & Co., Publishers, 1898), p. 625; Woodrow Wilson, *The New Freedom: A Call for the Emancipation of the Generous Energies of a People* (New York: Doubleday, Page & Company, 1913, 1918), pp. 20, 284.

108. Woodrow Wilson, *Congressional Government: A Study in American Politics* (Boston: Houghton Mifflin, 1885), pp. 8, 242–243;

Woodrow Wilson, *Constitutional Government in the United States* (New York: Columbia University Press, 1908), pp. 157, 158, 159, 160, 167, 168, 169, 192, 193, 194.

109. Woodrow Wilson, *The New Freedom*, pp. 19, 20, 261, 283, 284, 294.

110. See, for example, Angus Deaton, *The Great Escape: Health, Wealth, and the Origins of Inequality* (Princeton: Princeton University Press, 2013), p. 2. See also Robert A. Dahl and Charles E. Lindblom, *Politics, Economics, and Welfare: Planning and Politico-Economic Systems Resolved into Basic Social Processes* (Chicago: University of Chicago Press, 1976), pp. 29, 36, 49, 425, 518.

111. Edward Alsworth Ross, *Seventy Years of It*, pp. 97–98.

112. Roscoe Pound, "The Need of a Sociological Jurisprudence," *The Green Bag*, October 1907, pp. 614, 615.

113. Jonathan Peter Spiro, *Defending the Master Race*, pp. 6, 10, 17, 22, 23, 28, 31, 32.

114. Ibid., p. 17.

115. Ibid., p. 250.

116. Eligio R. Padilla and Gail E. Wyatt, "The Effects of Intelligence and Achievement Testing on Minority Group Children," *The Psychosocial Development of Minority Group Children*, edited by Gloria Johnson Powell, et al (New York: Brunner/Mazel, Publishers, 1983), p. 418.

117. H.H. Goddard, "The Binet Tests in Relation to Immigration," *Journal of Psycho-Asthenics*, Vol. 18, No. 2 (December 1913), p. 110.

118. N.J.G. Pounds, *An Historical Geography of Europe* (Cambridge: Cambridge University Press, 1990), p. 9.

119. Philip E. Vernon, *Intelligence and Cultural Environment*, pp. 101, 145, 157–158; Mandel Sherman and Cora B. Key, "The Intelligence of Isolated Mountain Children," *Child Development*, Vol. 3, No. 4 (December 1932), p. 284; [Robert M. Yerkes,] National Academy of Sciences, *Psychological Examining in the United States Army*, Vol. XV, Part III, p. 705. See also Thomas Sowell, *Intellectuals and Race*, pp. 67–68.

120. I.M. Stead, *Celtic Art in Britain before the Roman Conquest* (Cambridge, Massachusetts: Harvard University Press, 1985), p. 4.

121. Luigi Barzini, *The Europeans* (New York: Simon and Schuster, 1983), p. 47.

122. Joel Mokyr, *The Lever of Riches: Technological Creativity and Economic Progress* (New York: Oxford University Press, 1990), pp. 210–211, 214–218.

123. Andrew Tanzer, "The Bamboo Network," *Forbes*, July 8, 1994, p. 139; The Economist, *Pocket World in Figures: 1997 Edition* (London: Profile Books, 1996), p. 14.

124. U.S. Bureau of the Census, "Total Population," *2011–2015 American Community Survey*, 5-Year Estimates, Table B01003; U.S. Bureau of the Census, "Median Household Income in the Past 12 Months (In 2015 Inflation-Adjusted Dollars)," *2011–2015 American Community Survey*, 5-Year Estimates, Table B19013; U.S. Bureau of the Census, *2020 Poverty and Median Household Income Estimates— Counties, States, and National,* Small Area Income and Poverty Estimates (SAIPE) Program, Release date: December 2021; U.S. Bureau of the Census, "QuickFacts" for the following counties in Kentucky: Breathitt, Clay, Jackson, Lee, Leslie, Mogoffin, and Owsley, downloaded on November 15, 2022 and January 12, 2023; Emily A. Shrider, Melissa Kollar, Frances Chen and Jessica Semega, "Income and Poverty in the United States: 2020," *Current Population Reports*, P60–273, p. 27. See also Brett Barrouquere and Dylan T. Lovan, "Kentucky County Feels Food Stamp Reductions Sharply," *Washington Post*, February 2, 2014, p. A5; Annie Lowrey, "Bluegrass-State Blues," *New York Times Magazine*, June 29, 2014, p. 13.

125. Carl C. Brigham, *A Study of American Intelligence*, p. 29.

126. Ibid., p. xx.

127. Carl C. Brigham, "Intelligence Tests of Immigrant Groups," *Psychological Review*, Vol. 37, Issue 2 (March 1930), p. 165.

128. Rudolf Pintner, *Intelligence Testing: Methods and Results*, new edition (New York: Henry Holt and Company, 1931), p. 453;

Charles Murray, *Human Accomplishment: The Pursuit of Excellence in the Arts and Sciences, 800 B.C. to 1950* (New York: HarperCollins, 2003), pp. 291, 292; Malcolm Gladwell, "Getting In," *The New Yorker,* October 10, 2005, pp. 80–86.

129. Sandra Scarr and Richard A. Weinberg, "IQ Test Performance of Black Children Adopted by White Families," *American Psychologist* (October 1976), pp. 726, 732, 736.

130. James R. Flynn, "Massive IQ Gains in 14 Nations: What IQ Tests Really Measure," *Psychological Bulletin*, Vol. 101, No. 2 (1987), pp. 171–191. See also James R. Flynn, "The Mean IQ of Americans: Massive Gains 1932 to 1978," *Psychological Bulletin*, Vol. 95, No. 1 (1984), pp. 29–51.

131. Since IQ tests were often used to assess the mental level of children— and it would be unrealistic to expect six-year-olds to do as well on these tests as twelve-year-olds, each child's performance is compared to the average performance of children the same age. To do this, each child's raw score on an IQ test was called the child's "mental age." That mental age is then compared to the same child's chronological age by creating a fraction, with the child's mental age divided by that child's chronological age. The resulting quotient is then multiplied by 100, so that the resulting "intelligence quotient" (IQ) can be read as the percentage of the average performance of children the same age. Thus an IQ of 85 means that the individual correctly answered 85 percent of the questions answered by others in the same age bracket, and an IQ of 115 indicates that the individual correctly answered 15 percent more questions than others in the same age category. For adults, the IQ test score is no longer so directly linked with age but the intelligence quotient of a given individual is compared with that of other adults in general.

132. Lisa H. Trahan, et al., "The Flynn Effect: A Meta-Analysis," *Psychological Bulletin*, Vol. 140, No. 5 (2014), pp. 1332–1360; James R. Flynn, "The Mean IQ of Americans: Massive Gains 1932 to 1978," *Psychological Bulletin*, Vol. 95, No. 1 (1984), pp. 29–51.

133. James R. Flynn, *Where Have All the Liberals Gone? Race, Class, and Ideals in America* (Cambridge: Cambridge University Press, 2008), pp. 72–74.

134. Charles Murray, *Facing Reality: Two Truths About Race in America* (New York: Encounter Books, 2021), p. 38.

135. Gunnar Myrdal, *An American Dilemma: The Negro Problem and Modern Democracy* (New York: Harper & Brothers, 1944), p. 99. Belief that innate mental inferiority of black children had been proved was reported as "a common fallacy" by James B. Conant in 1961. James B. Conant, *Slums and Suburbs: A Commentary on Schools in Metropolitan Areas* (New York: McGraw-Hill, 1961), p. 12.

136. Arthur R. Jensen, *Genetics and Education* (New York: Harper & Row, 1972), pp. 43–44.

137. James R. Flynn, "The Mean IQ of Americans: Massive Gains 1932 to 1978," *Psychological Bulletin*, Vol. 95, No. 1 (1984), pp. 29–51; James R. Flynn, *Where Have All the Liberals Gone?*, pp. 72–74; James R. Flynn, "Massive IQ Gains in 14 Nations: What IQ Tests Really Measure," *Psychological Bulletin*, Vol. 101, No. 2 (1987), pp. 171–191.

138. Rochelle Sharpe, "Losing Ground: In Latest Recession, Only Blacks Suffered Net Employment Loss," *Wall Street Journal*, September 14, 1993, pp. A1, A12.

139. Glenn B. Canner, et al., "Home Mortgage Disclosure Act: Expanded Data on Residential Lending," *Federal Reserve Bulletin*, November 1991, p. 870; Glenn B. Canner and Dolores S. Smith, "Expanded HMDA Data on Residential Lending: One Year Later," *Federal Reserve Bulletin*, November 1992, p. 808.

140. Board of Governors of the Federal Reserve System, *Report to the Congress on Credit Scoring and Its Effects on the Availability and Affordability of Credit*, submitted to the Congress pursuant to Section 215 of the Fair and Accurate Credit Transactions Act of 2003, August 2007, p. 80.

141. Thomas Sowell, *The Housing Boom and Bust*, revised edition (New York: Basic Books, 2009), pp. 103–104; Alicia H. Munnell, et al., "Mortgage Lending in Boston: Interpreting HMDA Data," Federal Reserve Bank of Boston, Working Paper No. 92–7, October 1992, pp. 2, 25.

142. Thomas Sowell, *The Housing Boom and Bust*, revised edition, pp. 29, 30, 31, 36–44, 48, 51, 72–74, 77, 81–82, 100, 109.

143. Thomas Sowell, "Froth in Frisco or Another Bubble?" *Wall Street Journal*, May 26, 2005, p. A13.

144. Thomas Sowell, *The Housing Boom and Bust*, revised edition, Chapters 3 and 5; Dean Baker, *The Housing Bubble and the Great Recession: Ten Years Later*, Center for Economic and Policy Research, September 2018; Justin Lahart, "The Great Recession: A Downturn Sized Up," *Wall Street Journal*, July 28, 2009, p. A12; "No Place Like Home," *The Economist*, January 18, 2020, special report on housing, p. 3.

145. Bob Zelnick, *Backfire: A Reporter's Look at Affirmative Action* (Washington: Regnery Publishing, Inc., 1996), p. 330.

146. See the "Dear Colleague Letter" issued by the U.S. Department of Justice and U.S. Department of Education on January 8, 2014.

147. Abigail Thernstrom and Stephan Thernstrom, *No Excuses: Closing the Racial Gap in Learning* (New York: Simon and Schuster, 2004), pp. 138, 139.

148. Ibid., p. 140.

149. *The Martin Luther King, Jr. Companion: Quotations from the Speeches, Essays, and Books of Martin Luther King, Jr.*, selected by Coretta Scott King (New York: St. Martin's Press, 1993), p. 101.

CHAPTER 3: CHESS PIECES FALLACIES

1. John Rawls, *A Theory of Justice* (Cambridge, Massachusetts: Harvard University Press, 1971), pp. 30–31, 43, 60–61, 302, 325.

2. Adam Smith, *The Theory of Moral Sentiments* (Indianapolis: Liberty Classics, 1976), pp. 380–381.

3. Edmund Burke, *The Writings and Speeches of Edmund Burke*, Volume II: *Party, Parliament, and the American Crisis 1766–1774*, edited by Paul Langford (New York: Oxford University Press, 1981), p. 459.

4. "Maryland's Mobile Millionaires," *Wall Street Journal*, March 12, 2010, p. A18.

5. "Ducking Higher Taxes," *Wall Street Journal*, December 21, 2010, p. A18.

6. David Walker and Mike Foster, "New U.K. Tax Sends Hedge Funds Fleeing," *Wall Street Journal*, August 25, 2009, p. C2.

7. "Iceland's Laffer Curve," *Wall Street Journal*, March 12, 2007, p. A14.

8. Andrew W. Mellon, *Taxation: The People's Business* (New York: The Macmillan Company, 1924), p. 74; Robert A. Wilson, "Personal Exemptions and Individual Income Tax Rates, 1913–2002," *Statistics of Income Bulletin*, Spring 2002, p. 219.

9. Robert A. Wilson, "Personal Exemptions and Individual Income Tax Rates, 1913–2002," *Statistics of Income Bulletin*, Spring 2002, p. 219; Gene Smiley and Richard H. Keehn, "Federal Personal Income Tax Policy in the 1920s," *Journal of Economic History*, Vol. 55, No. 2 (June 1995), pp. 286, 295; United States Internal Revenue Service, *Statistics of Income: 1920* (Washington: Government Printing Office, 1922), p. 5; United States Internal Revenue Service, *Statistics of Income: 1928* (Washington: Government Printing Office, 1930), p. 5.

10. Andrew W. Mellon, *Taxation*, pp. 13, 79, 80, 94, 127–128, and Chapter VIII.

11. "Text of President's Speech Elaborating His Views," *Washington Post*, February 13, 1924, p. 4; Andrew W. Mellon, *Taxation*, pp. 17, 20–21, 80, 150–151.

12. Andrew W. Mellon, *Taxation*, p. 170.

13. Gene Smiley and Richard H. Keehn, "Federal Personal Income Tax Policy in the 1920s," *Journal of Economic History*, Vol. 55, No. 2 (June 1995), p. 289. See also Andrew W. Mellon, *Taxation*, pp. 79–80, 141.

14. See, for example, my monograph, "'Trickle Down Theory' and 'Tax Cuts for the Rich'" (Stanford: Hoover Institution Press, 2012).

15. Robert A. Wilson, "Personal Exemptions and Individual Income Tax Rates, 1913–2002," *Statistics of Income Bulletin*, Spring 2002, p. 219; United States Internal Revenue Service, *Statistics of Income: 1920*, p. 5; United States Internal Revenue Service, *Statistics of Income: 1928*, p. 5.

16. See, for example, Joseph A. Schumpeter, *History of Economic Analysis* (New York: Oxford University Press, 1954), Part II.

17. Henry Hazlitt, *The Wisdom of Henry Hazlitt* (Irvington-on-Hudson, New York: The Foundation for Economic Education, 1993), p. 329.

18. Peter Robinson, "A Capital Thinker," *Stanford Magazine*, January/February 2007, p. 47.

19. William N. Walker, "Nixon Taught Us How Not to Fight Inflation," *Wall Street Journal*, August 14, 2021, p. A13.

20. Michael Wines, "Caps on Prices Only Deepen Zimbabweans' Misery," *New York Times*, August 2, 2007, pp. A1, A8.

21. See, for example, Robert L. Schuettinger and Eamonn F. Butler, *Forty Centuries of Wage and Price Controls: How Not to Fight Inflation* (Washington: Heritage Foundation, 1979); Thomas Sowell, *Basic Economics: A Common Sense Guide to the Economy*, fifth edition (New York: Basic Books, 2015), Chapter 3.

22. See Thomas Sowell, *Basic Economics*, fifth edition, pp. 1, 39–48, 49.

23. Thomas Sowell, *Discrimination and Disparities*, revised and enlarged edition (New York: Basic Books, 2019), pp. 52–55, 105–110; Thomas Sowell, *Basic Economics*, fifth edition, Chapter 11.

24. Walter E. Williams, *Race & Economics: How Much Can Be Blamed on Discrimination* (Stanford: Hoover Institution Press, 2011), p. 42.

25. Ibid., pp. 42–43.

26. George J. Stigler, "The Economics of Minimum Wage Legislation," *American Economic Review*, Vol. 36, No. 3 (June 1946), p. 358.

27. Walter E. Williams, *Race & Economics*, pp. 42–43.

28. Alison Stewart, *First Class: The Legacy of Dunbar, America's First Black Public High School* (Chicago: Lawrence Hill Books, 2013), Chapter 10; Frederick W. Gooding, Jr., *American Dream Deferred: Back Federal Workers in Washington, DC, 1941–1981* (Pittsburgh: University of Pittsburgh Press, 2018), pp. 101–105, 107–109, 111, 113–115. See also Thomas Sowell, *A Personal Odyssey* (New York: The Free Press, 2000), p. 110.

29. Milton & Rose Friedman, *Free to Choose: A Personal Statement* (New York: Harcourt Brace Jovanovich, 1980), p. 238.

30. Gary S. Becker, *The Economics of Discrimination,* second edition (Chicago: University of Chicago Press, 1971).

31. See, for example, Thomas Sowell, *Discrimination and Disparities,* revised and enlarged edition, pp. 49–52. The term "Discrimination II," used in those pages, was defined and illustrated on pages 30–33.

32. Bernard E. Anderson, *Negro Employment in Public Utilities: A Study of Racial Policies in the Electric Power, Gas, and Telephone Industries* (Philadelphia: University of Pennsylvania Press, 1970); Venus Green, *Race on the Line: Gender, Labor, and Technology in the Bell System, 1880–1980* (Durham: Duke University Press, 2001), pp. 210–211; Michael R. Winston, "Through the Back Door: Academic Racism and the Negro Scholar in Historical Perspective," *Daedalus*, Vol. 100, No. 3 (Summer 1971), pp. 695, 705; Milton & Rose Friedman, *Two Lucky People: Memoirs* (Chicago: University of Chicago Press, 1998), pp. 91–92, 94–95, 105–106, 153–154; Greg Robinson, "Davis, Allison," *Encyclopedia of African-American Culture and History*, edited by Colin A. Palmer (Detroit: Thomson-Gale, 2006), Volume C–F, p. 583; "The Talented Black Scholars Whom No White University Would Hire," *Journal of Blacks in Higher Education*, No. 58 (Winter 2007/2008), p. 81; Thomas Sowell, *Discrimination and Disparities,* revised and enlarged edition, pp. 49–52; Thomas Sowell, *Race and Economics* (New York: David McKay Company, Inc., 1975), pp. 182–183.

33. See, for example, Bernard E. Anderson, *Negro Employment in Public Utilities*, pp. 73, 80, 84–87, 92–95, 114, 139, 150, 152; Venus Green, *Race on the Line*, pp. 210–211; Michael R. Winston, "Through the Back Door: Academic Racism and the Negro Scholar in Historical

Perspective," *Daedalus*, Vol. 100, No. 3 (Summer 1971), pp. 695, 705; Greg Robinson, "Davis, Allison," *Encyclopedia of African-American Culture and History*, edited by Colin A. Palmer, Volume C–F, p. 583; "The Talented Black Scholars Whom No White University Would Hire," *Journal of Blacks in Higher Education*, No. 58 (Winter 2007/2008), p. 81; Thomas Sowell, *Discrimination and Disparities*, revised and enlarged edition, pp. 49–52; Thomas Sowell, *Race and Economics*, pp. 182–183.

34. Bernard E. Anderson, *Negro Employment in Public Utilities;* Venus Green, *Race on the Line*, pp. 210–211; Michael R. Winston, "Through the Back Door: Academic Racism and the Negro Scholar in Historical Perspective," *Daedalus*, Vol. 100, No. 3 (Summer 1971), pp. 695, 705; Milton & Rose Friedman, *Two Lucky People*, pp. 91–92, 94–95, 105–106, 153–154; Greg Robinson, "Davis, Allison," *Encyclopedia of African-American Culture and History*, edited by Colin A. Palmer, Volume C–F, p. 583; "The Talented Black Scholars Whom No White University Would Hire," *Journal of Blacks in Higher Education*, No. 58 (Winter 2007/2008), p. 81; Thomas Sowell, *Discrimination and Disparities*, revised and enlarged edition, pp. 49–52; Thomas Sowell, *Race and Economics*, pp. 182–183.

35. "The Talented Black Scholars Whom No White University Would Hire," *Journal of Blacks in Higher Education*, No. 58 (Winter 2007/2008), p. 81; Michael R. Winston, "Through the Back Door: Academic Racism and the Negro Scholar in Historical Perspective," *Daedalus*, Vol. 100, No. 3 (Summer 1971), p. 705.

36. Ezra Mendelsohn, *The Jews of East Central Europe Between the World Wars* (Bloomington: Indiana University Press, 1983), pp. 23, 27.

37. Raphael Mahler, "Jews in Public Service and the Liberal Professions in Poland, 1918–1939," *Jewish Social Studies*, Vol. 6, No. 4 (October 1944), pp. 298, 299.

38. Walter E. Williams, *South Africa's War Against Capitalism* (New York: Praeger Publishers, 1989), pp. 78, 101–105.

39. Ibid., p. 81.

40. "Class and the American Dream," *New York Times*, May 30, 2005, p. A14.

41. Eugene Robinson, "Tattered Dream: Who'll Tackle the Issue of Upward Mobility?" *Washington Post*, November 23, 2007, p. A39.

42. E.J. Dionne, Jr., "Political Stupidity, U.S. Style," *Washington Post*, July 29, 2010, p. A23. This column also appeared in *Investor's Business Daily*, under the title "Overtaxed Rich Is a Fairy Tale of Supply Side."

43. *Public Papers of the Presidents of the United States, Barack Obama: 2013* (Washington: United States Government Publishing Office, 2018), Book II, p. 1331.

44. Joseph E. Stiglitz, *The Great Divide: Unequal Societies and What We Can Do About Them* (New York: W.W. Norton, 2015), p. 88.

45. Ibid., p. 90.

46. Ibid., p. xv.

47. U.S. Department of the Treasury, "Income Mobility in the U.S. from 1996 to 2005," November 13, 2007, p. 7.

48. See, for example, W. Michael Cox and Richard Alm, "By Our Own Bootstraps: Economic Opportunity & the Dynamics of Income Distribution," *Annual Report, 1995*, Federal Reserve Bank of Dallas, p. 8; Mark Robert Rank, Thomas A. Hirschl and Kirk A. Foster, *Chasing the American Dream: Understanding What Shapes Our Fortunes* (Oxford: Oxford University Press, 2014), p. 105; Thomas A. Hirschl and Mark R. Rank, "The Life Course Dynamics of Affluence," *PLoS ONE*, January 28, 2015, p. 5.

49. Thomas A. Hirschl and Mark R. Rank, "The Life Course Dynamics of Affluence," *PLoS ONE*, January 28, 2015, p. 5.

50. W. Michael Cox and Richard Alm, "By Our Own Bootstraps: Economic Opportunity & the Dynamics of Income Distribution," *Annual Report, 1995*, Federal Reserve Bank of Dallas, p. 8.

51. Ibid.

52. Ibid.

53. U.S. Department of the Treasury, "Income Mobility in the U.S. from 1996 to 2005," November 13, 2007, p. 10. See also "Movin' On Up," *Wall Street Journal*, November 13, 2007, p. A24.

54. Niels Veldhuis, et al., "The 'Poor' Are Getting Richer," *Fraser Forum*, January/February 2013, p. 25.

55. U.S. Bureau of Labor Statistics, "Consumer Expenditures Report," Report 1090, December 2020, Table 1, p. 12.

56. Ibid.

57. John McNeil, "Changes in Median Household Income: 1969 to 1996," *Current Population Reports*, P23–196 (Washington: U.S. Bureau of the Census, 1998), p. 1.

58. Herman P. Miller, *Income Distribution in the United States* (Washington: U.S. Government Printing Office, 1966), p. 7.

59. Louis Uchitelle, "Stagnant Pay: A Delayed Impact," *New York Times*, June 18, 1991, p. D2.

60. Barbara Vobejda, "Elderly Lead All in Financial Improvement," *Washington Post*, September 1, 1998, p. A3.

61. Amy Kaslow, "Growing American Economy Leaves Middle Class Behind," *Christian Science Monitor*, November 1, 1994, p. 2.

62. Compare Tom Wicker, "L.B.J.'s Great Society," *New York Times*, May 7, 1990, p. A15; Tom Wicker, "Let 'Em Eat Swiss Cheese," *New York Times*, September 2, 1988, p. A27.

63. Paul Krugman, "Rich Man's Recovery," *New York Times*, September 13, 2013, p. A25.

64. U.S. Department of the Treasury, "Income Mobility in the U.S. from 1996 to 2005," November 13, 2007, p. 4.

65. Internal Revenue Service, Statistics of Income Division, "The 400 Individual Income Tax Returns Reporting the Largest Adjusted Gross Incomes Each Year, 1992–2014," December 2016, Table 4, p. 17.

66. Emily A. Shrider, Melissa Kollar, Frances Chen and Jessica Semega, "Income and Poverty in the United States: 2020," *Current Population Reports*, P60–273 (Washington: U.S. Government Publishing Office, 2021), p. 9.

67. Joseph E. Stiglitz, *The Great Divide*, p. xv.

68. Alan Reynolds, *Income and Wealth* (Westport, Connecticut: Greenwood Press, 2006), p. 67.

69. Robert Rector and Rachel Sheffield, "Air Conditioning, Cable TV, and an Xbox: What Is Poverty in the United States Today?" *Backgrounder*, No. 2575, Heritage Foundation, July 18, 2011, p. 10.

70. Thomas A. Hirschl and Mark R. Rank, "The Life Course Dynamics of Affluence," *PLoS ONE*, January 28, 2015, p. 5.

71. W. Michael Cox and Richard Alm, "By Our Own Bootstraps: Economic Opportunity & the Dynamics of Income Distribution," *Annual Report, 1995*, Federal Reserve Bank of Dallas, p. 16; U.S. Bureau of the Census, "Age— All People (Both Sexes Combined) by Median and Mean Income: 1974 to 2020," *Current Population Survey, 1975–2021*, Annual Social and Economic Supplements (CPS ASEC), Table P–10.

72. Alan Reynolds, *Income and Wealth*, p. 22.

CHAPTER 4: KNOWLEDGE FALLACIES

1. See, for example, Thomas Sowell, *A Conflict of Visions: Ideological Origins of Political Struggles* (New York: Basic Books, 2002), Chapter 3.

2. Joses C. Moya, *Cousins and Strangers: Spanish Immigrants in Buenos Aires, 1850–1930* (Berkeley: University of California Press, 1998), pp. 119, 145–146. Similarly, most of the Italian immigrants to Australia, between 1881 and 1899, came from places containing only 10 percent of the population of Italy. Helen Ware, *A Profile of the Italian Community in Australia* (Melbourne: Australian Institute of Multicultural Affairs and Co.As.It. Italian Assistance Association, 1981), p. 12.

3. Helen Ware, *A Profile of the Italian Community in Australia*, p. 12.

4. G. Cresciani, "Italian Immigrants 1920–1945," *The Australian People: An Encyclopedia of the Nation, Its People and Their Origins*, edited by James Jupp (Cambridge: Cambridge University Press, 2001), p. 501.

5. Walter D. Kamphoefner, "The German Agricultural Frontier: Crucible or Cocoon," *Ethnic Forum*, Volume 4, Nos. 1–2 (Spring 1984), pp. 24–25.

6. Theodore Huebener, *The Germans in America* (Philadelphia: Chilton Company, 1962), p. 84; Hildegard Binder Johnson, "The Location of German Immigrants in the Middle West," *Annals of the Association of American Geographers*, edited by Henry Madison Kendall, Volume XLI (1951), pp. 24–25.

7. Jack Chen, *The Chinese of America* (San Francisco: Harper & Row, 1980), p. 18.

8. Louise L'Estrange Fawcett, "Lebanese, Palestinians and Syrians in Colombia," *The Lebanese in the World: A Century of Emigration*, edited by Albert Hourani and Nadim Shehadi (London: The Centre for Lebanese Studies, 1992), p. 368.

9. Moses Rischin, *The Promised City: New York's Jews 1870–1914* (Cambridge, Massachusetts: Harvard University Press, 1962), pp. 76, 78.

10. Tyler Anbinder, *City of Dreams: The 400-Year Epic History of Immigrant New York* (Boston: Houghton Mifflin Harcourt, 2016), p. 185.

11. Charles A. Price, *The Methods and Statistics of 'Southern Europeans in Australia'* (Canberra: The Australian National University, 1963), p. 45.

12. John Rawls, *A Theory of Justice* (Cambridge, Massachusetts: Harvard University Press, 1971), pp. 30–31, 43, 60–61, 302, 325.

13. Frederick Jackson Turner, "Pioneer Ideals and the State University," *Rereading Frederick Jackson Turner: "The Significance of the*

Frontier in American History" and Other Essays, edited by John Mack Faragher (New York: Henry Holt, 1994), p. 116.

14. F.A. Hayek, *The Constitution of Liberty* (Chicago: University of Chicago Press, 1960), p. 26.

15. John Rawls, *A Theory of Justice,* pp. 30–31, 43, 60–61, 302, 325.

16. Ibid.

17. See John Dewey, "Can Education Share in Social Reconstruction?" *John Dewey: The Later Works, 1925–1953,* Volume 9: *1933–1934,* edited by Jo Ann Boydston (Carbondale: Southern Illinois University Press, 1986), pp. 205–209.

18. Jean-Jacques Rousseau, *The Social Contract,* translated by Maurice Cranston (New York: Penguin Books, 1968), p. 69.

19. William Godwin, *Enquiry Concerning Political Justice, and Its Influence on General Virtue and Happiness* (London: G.G.J. and J. Robinson, 1793). The word "Political" in the title was used in the sense common at the time, referring to organized society— the polity— much as the expression "political economy"in that same era referred to the economics of the society or polity, as distinguished from the economics of a household or a business. In short, Godwin wrote on social justice, as that term is used today.

20. William Godwin, *Enquiry Concerning Political Justice, and Its Influence on Morals and Happiness,* edited by F.E.L. Priestley (Toronto: University of Toronto Press, 1946), Vol. I, p. 104.

21. John Stuart Mill, *Principles of Political Economy,* edited by W.J. Ashley (New York: Longmans, Green and Company, 1909), p. 947.

22. John Stuart Mill, "On Liberty," *Collected Works of John Stuart Mill,* Vol. XVIII: *Essays on Politics and Society,* edited by J.M. Robson (Toronto: University of Toronto Press, 1977), p. 269.

23. John Stuart Mill, "Civilization," Ibid., p. 139.

24. Ibid., p. 121.

25. John Stuart Mill, "De Tocqueville on Democracy in America [I]," Ibid., p. 86.

26. John Stuart Mill, "On Liberty," Ibid., p. 222.

27. Ibid. p. 267.

28. John Stuart Mill, "Civilization," Ibid., p. 128.

29. Randall E. Stross, *The Wizard of Menlo Park: How Thomas Alva Edison Invented the Modern World* (New York: Crown, 2007), p. 4; Ford Richardson Bryan, *Beyond the Model T: The Other Ventures of Henry Ford*, revised edition (Detroit: Wayne State University Press, 1997), p. 175.

30. Peter L. Jakab, *Visions of a Flying Machine: The Wright Brothers and the Process of Invention* (Washington: Smithsonian Institution Press, 1990), pp. 2–3, 7.

31. Jean-Jacques Rousseau, *The Social Contract*, translated by Maurice Cranston, p. 115.

32. Ibid., p. 89.

33. William Godwin, *Enquiry Concerning Political Justice, and Its Influence on Morals and Happiness*, edited by F.E.L. Priestley, Vol. I, p. 446; Antoine-Nicolas de Condorcet, *Sketch for a Historical Picture of the Progress of the Human Mind*, translated by June Barraclough (London: Weidenfeld and Nicolson, 1955), p. 114.

34. Karl Marx and Frederick Engels, *Selected Correspondence: 1846–1895* (New York: International Publishers, 1942), p. 190.

35. Bernard Shaw, *The Intelligent Woman's Guide to Socialism and Capitalism* (London: Constable and Company, 1928), p. 456.

36. Ronald Dworkin, *Taking Rights Seriously* (Cambridge, Massachusetts: Harvard University Press, 1978), p. 239.

37. Mona Charen, *Do-Gooders: How Liberals Hurt Those They Claim to Help— and the Rest of Us* (New York: Sentinel, 2004), p. 124.

38. Ralph Nader, "The Safe Car You Can't Buy," *The Nation*, April 11, 1959, p. 312.

39. Milton & Rose Friedman, *Two Lucky People: Memoirs* (Chicago: University of Chicago Press, 1998), p. 454.

40. George J. Stigler, *Memoirs of an Unregulated Economist* (New York: Basic Books, 1988), p. 89.

41. Ibid., p. 178.

42. Milton & Rose Friedman, *Two Lucky People*, pp. 370–371.

43. John Maynard Keynes, *Two Memoirs: Dr. Melchoir, A Defeated Enemy and My Early Beliefs* (London: Rupert Hart-Davis, 1949), pp. 97–98.

44. Ibid., p. 98.

45. R.F. Harrod, *The Life of John Maynard Keynes* (London: Macmillan, 1952), p. 468.

46. Walter E. Weyl, *The New Democracy: An Essay on Certain Political and Economic Tendencies in the United States* (New York: The Macmillan Company, 1912), pp. 164, 353.

47. Ibid., p. 164.

48. Walter E. Williams, *Race & Economics: How Much Can Be Blamed on Discrimination* (Stanford: Hoover Institution Press, 2011), pp. 42–43.

49. Ibid.

50. Ibid., p. 43.

51. Nicholas Kristof, "Is a Hard Life Inherited?" *New York Times*, August 10, 2014, Sunday Review section, p. 1.

52. See, for examples, Thomas Sowell, *Basic Economics: A Common Sense Guide to the Economy*, fifth edition (New York: Basic Books, 2015), Chapter 11; Thomas Sowell, *Discrimination and Disparities*, revised and enlarged edition (New York: Basic Books, 2019), pp. 52–55, 105–110; P.T. Bauer, "Regulated Wages in Under-developed Countries," *The Public Stake in Union Power*, edited by Philip D. Bradley (Charlottesville: University of Virginia Press, 1959), pp. 324–349; Walter E. Williams, *Race & Economics*, pp. 32–38, 46–48, 51–53.

53. "Economic and Financial Indicators," *The Economist*, March 15, 2003, p. 100.

54. "Economic and Financial Indicators," *The Economist*, September 7, 2013, p. 92.

55. "Hong Kong's Jobless Rate Falls," *Wall Street Journal*, January 16, 1991, p. C16.

56. U. S. Bureau of the Census, *Historical Statistics of the United States: Colonial Times to 1970* (Washington: Government Printing Office, 1975), Part 1, p. 126.

57. Charles H. Young and Helen R. Y. Reid, *The Japanese Canadians* (Toronto: University of Toronto Press, 1938), pp. 47–50; Tomoko Makabe, "The Theory of the Split Labor Market: A Comparison of the Japanese Experience in Brazil and Canada," *Social Forces*, March 1981, pp. 795, 796.

58. Walter E. Williams, *South Africa's War Against Capitalism* (New York: Praeger Publishers, 1989), pp. 70–74; Walter E. Williams, *Race & Economics*, pp. 46–48; Walter E. Williams, *The State Against Blacks* (New York: New Press, 1982), pp. 39–40.

59. P.T. Bauer, "Regulated Wages in Under-developed Countries," *The Public Stake in Union Power*, edited by Philip D. Bradley, pp. 324–349; Walter E. Williams, *Race & Economics*, pp. 32–38. For a more general discussion of minimum wage laws and their effects on unemployment, see Thomas Sowell, *Basic Economics*, fifth edition, pp. 213–215, 220–233; Thomas Sowell, *Discrimination and Disparities*, revised and enlarged edition, pp. 52–55, 105–110.

60. Yuka Hayashi and Lalita Clozel, "CFPB Reveals Its Plan to Overhaul Payday-Lending Regulation," *Wall Street Journal*, February 7, 2019, p. B11.

61. For examples, see the following editorials from the *New York Times*: "391 Percent Payday Loan," April 13, 2009, p. A20, "Pay Pals," June 10, 2009, p. A28, and "Borrowers Bled Dry," July 13, 2009, p. A18.

62. See, for example, "Payday Parasites," *Washington Post*, February 14, 2008, p. A24; Bethany McLean, "Loan Shark Inc.," *The Atlantic Monthly*, May 2016, pp. 64–69; "A Crackdown on Predatory

Payday Loans," *Los Angeles Times,* October 9, 2017, p. A13; "Payday Lenders, Unleashed," *Los Angeles Times,* February 8, 2019, p. A10.

63. Irving Howe, *World of Our Fathers: The Journey of the East European Jews to America and the Life They Found and Made* (New York: Harcourt Brace Jovanovich, 1976), p. 148.

64. Simon Kuznets, "Immigration of Russian Jews to the United States: Background and Structure," *Perspectives in American History,* edited by Donald Fleming and Bernard Bailyn (Cambridge, Massachusetts: Charles Warren Center for Studies in American History, Harvard University, 1975), Vol. IX, p. 113.

65. Oliver MacDonagh, "The Irish Famine Emigration to the United States," *Perspectives in American History,* edited by Donald Fleming and Bernard Bailyn (Cambridge, Massachusetts: Charles Warren Center for Studies in American History, Harvard University, 1976), Vol. X, pp. 394–395.

66. Walter E. Weyl, *The New Democracy,* p. 164.

67. United States Senate, Eighty-Ninth Congress, Second Session, *Family Planning Program: Hearing Before the Subcommittee on Employment, Manpower and Poverty of the Committee on Labor and Public Welfare* (Washington: U. S. Government Printing Office, 1966), p. 84.

68. The *New York Times* editorially rejected "emotions and unexamined tradition" in this area, and its education editor declared: "To fear that sex education will become synonymous with greater sexual permissiveness is to misunderstand the fundamental purpose of the entire enterprise." Fred M. Hechinger, "Introduction," *Sex Education and the Schools,* edited by Virginia Hilu (New York: Harper & Row, 1967), p. xiv. See also "Three's a Crowd," *New York Times,* March 17, 1972, p. 40.

69. The American Social Health Association, *Today's VD Control Problem* (New York: American Social Health Association, 1966), Table 1, p. 20.

70. Jacqueline R. Kasun, *The War Against Population: The Economics and Ideology of World Population Control* (San Francisco: Ignatius Press, 1988), p. 142.

71. Hearings Before the Select Committee on Population, Ninety-Fifth Congress, Second Session, *Fertility and Contraception in America: Adolescent and Pre-Adolescent Pregnancy* (Washington: U.S. Government Printing Office, 1978), Volume II, p. 253.

72. Centers for Disease Control and Prevention, U.S. Department of Health and Human Services, *Sexually Transmitted Disease Surveillance 2019* (April 2021), p. 33.

73. Jacqueline R. Kasun, *The War Against Population*, pp. 142, 144.

74. Centers for Disease Control and Prevention, U.S. Department of Health and Human Services, "Births to Teenagers in the United States, 1940–2000," *National Vital Statistics Reports*, Vol. 49, No. 10 (September 25, 2001), Table 1, p. 10.

75. Ibid. See also graphs on page 2.

76. Marvin Zelnik and John F. Kantner, "Sexual and Contraceptive Experience of Young Unmarried Women in the United States, 1976 and 1971," *Family Planning Perspectives*, Vol. 9, No. 2 (March-April 1977), p. 56.

77. Suzanne Fields, "'War' Pits Parents vs. Public Policy," *Chicago Sun-Times*, October 17, 1992, p. 19.

78. Ibid.

79. James Hottois and Neal A. Milner, *The Sex Education Controversy: A Study of Politics, Education, and Morality* (Lexington, Massachusetts: Lexington Books, 1975), p. 6.

80. See, for example, Hearings Before the Select Committee on Population, Ninety-Fifth Congress, Second Session, *Fertility and Contraception in America*, Volume II, pp. 1, 2; Paul A. Reichelt and Harriet H. Werley, "Contraception, Abortion and Venereal Disease: Teenagers' Knowledge and the Effect of Education," *Family Planning Perspectives*, Vol. 7, No. 2 (March-April 1975), pp. 83–88; Les Picker, "Human Sexuality Education: Implications

for Biology Teaching," *The American Biology Teacher*, Vol. 46, No. 2 (February 1984), pp. 92–98.

81. Hearings Before the Select Committee on Population, Ninety-Fifth Congress, Second Session, *Fertility and Contraception in America*, Volume II, p. 625.

82. William Godwin, *Enquiry Concerning Political Justice, and Its Influence on Morals and Happiness*, edited by F.E.L. Priestley, Vol. I, p. 47.

83. William Godwin, *The Enquirer: Reflections on Education, Manners, and Literature* (London: G. G. and J. Robinson, 1797), p. 70.

84. Woodrow Wilson, "What is Progress?" *American Progressivism: A Reader*, edited by Ronald J. Pestritto and William J. Atto (Lanham, Maryland: Lexington Books, 2008), p. 48.

85. John Dewey, *Democracy and Education: An Introduction to the Philosophy of Education* (New York: The Macmillan Company, 1916), p. 92.

86. John Dewey and Evelyn Dewey, *Schools of To-Morrow* (New York: E.P. Dutton & Company, 1915), p. 304.

87. John Dewey, *Democracy and Education*, p. 24.

88. See, for example, Robert B. Westbrook, "Schools for Industrial Democrats: The Social Origins of John Dewey's Philosophy of Education," *American Journal of Education*, Vol. 100, No. 4 (August 1992), pp. 401–419.

89. Woodrow Wilson, "The Study of Administration," *Political Science Quarterly*, Vol. 2, No. 2 (June 1887), p. 207.

90. Ibid., p. 208.

91. Ibid., p. 214.

92. Ronald J. Pestritto and William J. Atto, "Introduction to American Progressivism," *American Progressivism*, edited by Ronald J. Pestritto and William J. Atto, pp. 23–25.

93. Woodrow Wilson, *The New Freedom: A Call for the Emancipation of the Generous Energies of a People* (New York: Doubleday, Page & Company, 1918, 1913), pp. vii–viii, 294. See also pages 19–20, 261, 283–284.

94. Ibid., p. v.

95. Ramsey Clark, *Crime in America: Observations On Its Nature, Causes, Prevention and Control* (New York: Simon and Schuster, 1970), p. 60.

96. Robert A. Dahl and Charles E. Lindblom, *Politics, Economics, and Welfare: Planning and Politico-Economic Systems Resolved into Basic Social Processes* (Chicago: University of Chicago Press, 1976), p. 36.

97. Ibid., p. 29.

98. Angus Deaton, *The Great Escape: Health, Wealth, and the Origins of Inequality* (Princeton: Princeton University Press, 2013), p. 2.

99. John Dewey, "Freedom and Culture," *John Dewey: The Later Works, 1925–1953*, Volume 13: *1938–1939*, edited by Jo Ann Boydston (Carbondale: Southern Illinois University Press, 1988), p. 65.

100. Ibid.

101. Ibid., p. 66.

102. John Dewey, *Reconstruction in Philosophy* (New York: Henry Holt and Company, 1920), p. 145.

103. John Dewey, *Democracy and Education*, p. 92.

104. Ibid., p. 369.

105. John Dewey, "Liberalism and Social Action," *John Dewey: The Later Works, 1925–1953*, Volume 11: *1935–1937*, edited by Jo Ann Boydston (Carbondale: Southern Illinois University Press, 1987), p. 53.

106. John Dewey and Evelyn Dewey, *Schools of To-Morrow*, p. 109.

107. Roscoe Pound, "The Need of a Sociological Jurisprudence," *The Green Bag*, October 1907, pp. 614, 615.

108. Roscoe Pound, *Criminal Justice in the American City: A Summary* (The Cleveland Foundation, 1922), Part VII, pp. 4, 13, 14, 29, 30, 31; Roscoe Pound, *Law and Morals* (Chapel Hill: North Carolina University Press, 1924), pp. ii, iii, 6, 33, 44, 59.

109. Roscoe Pound, *Law and Morals*, pp. 13, 14.

110. Roscoe Pound, *The Ideal Element in Law* (Indianapolis: Liberty Fund, 2002), pp. 19, 45, 104, 108, 110, 207, 258–259, 313.

111. Roscoe Pound, *Criminal Justice in the American City*, Part VII, pp. 5, 51; Roscoe Pound, "The Theory of Judicial Decision. III. A Theory of Judicial Decision for Today," *Harvard Law Review*, Vol. 36, No. 8 (June 1923), pp. 954, 955, 956, 957, 958.

112. Roscoe Pound, "The Need of a Sociological Jurisprudence," *The Green Bag*, October 1907, pp. 612, 613.

113. Barry Cushman, "Federalism," *The Cambridge Companion to the United States Constitution*, edited by Karen Orren and John W. Compton (New York: Cambridge University Press, 2018), p. 216.

114. Herbert Croly, a leading Progressive author and the first editor of *The New Republic* magazine, deplored what he called "the practical immutability of the Constitution." Herbert Croly, *The Promise of American Life* (New York: The Macmillan Company, 1912, 1909), p. 200.

115. Roscoe Pound, "The Theory of Judicial Decision. III. A Theory of Judicial Decision for Today," *Harvard Law Review*, Vol. 36, No. 8 (June 1923), p. 946.

116. Roscoe Pound, "Mechanical Jurisprudence," *Columbia Law Review*, Vol. 8, No. 8 (December 1908), p. 615.

117. Ibid., pp. 605, 609, 612.

118. Roscoe Pound, *Law and Morals*, pp. 55–56, 58; Roscoe Pound, "The Theory of Judicial Decision. III. A Theory of Judicial Decision for Today," *Harvard Law Review*, Vol. 36, No. 8 (June 1923), pp. 950, 953.

119. Roscoe Pound, "Mechanical Jurisprudence," *Columbia Law Review*, Vol. 8, No. 8 (December 1908), pp. 612, 614.

120. Godwin, Condorcet and some latter-day believers in that approach are quoted in Thomas Sowell, *A Conflict of Visions*, pp. 157–161, 197.

121. Louis D. Brandeis, "The Living Law," *Illinois Law Review*, Vol. 10, No. 7 (February 1916), p. 462; John Dewey, *Human Nature and Conduct: An Introduction to Social Psychology* (New York: Henry Holt and Company, 1922), pp. 18–19, 46; Roscoe Pound, "Review: *The Principles of Anthropology and Sociology in Their Relation to Criminal Procedure* by Maurice Parmelee," *American Political Science Review*, Vol. 3, No. 2 (May 1909), pp. 283–284.

122. See Fred P. Graham, "High Court Puts New Curb on Powers of the Police to Interrogate Suspects," *New York Times*, June 14, 1966, pp. 1, 25.

123. Sidney E. Zion, "Attack on Court Heard by Warren," *New York Times*, September 10, 1965, pp. 1, 38.

124. U. S. Bureau of the Census, *Historical Statistics of the United States*, Part 1, p. 414.

125. Ibid.; U.S. Bureau of the Census, *Statistical Abstract of the United States: 1980* (Washington: Government Printing Office, 1980), p. 186.

126. See U.S. Bureau of the Census, *Statistical Abstract of the United States: 1982–83* (Washington: Government Printing Office, 1982), p. 178.

127. Chief Justice Earl Warren, *The Memoirs of Earl Warren* (Garden City, New York: Doubleday and Company, Inc., 1977), p. 317. Such a reaction was not peculiar to Chief Justice Earl Warren. As far back as the eighteenth century, Edmund Burke saw a similar pattern among some of his contemporaries: "They never had any kind of system right or wrong, but only invented occasionally some miserable tale for the day, in order meanly to sneak out of difficulties into which they had proudly strutted." Edmund Burke, *Speeches and Letters on American Affairs* (London: J.M. Dent and Sons, Ltd., 1961), p. 8.

128. F.A. Hayek, *The Constitution of Liberty*, p. 30.

CHAPTER 5: WORDS, DEEDS AND DANGERS

1. Lionel Trilling, *The Liberal Imagination: Essays on Literature and Society* (Garden City, New York: Anchor Books, 1953), pp. 214–215.

2. Milton and Rose Friedman, *Free to Choose: A Personal Statement* (New York: Harcourt Brace Jovanovich, 1980), p. 146.

3. Friedrich Hayek, *Law, Legislation and Liberty: A New Statement of the Liberal Principles of Justice and Political Economy*, Vol. II: *The Mirage of Social Justice* (Chicago: University of Chicago Press, 1976), p. 64.

4. Ibid., p. 95; See also pp. 64, 75, 79; Friedrich Hayek, *Law, Legislation and Liberty: A New Statement of the Liberal Principles of Justice and Political Economy*, Vol. I: *Rules and Order* (Chicago: University of Chicago Press, 1973), p. 27.

5. Friedrich Hayek, *Law, Legislation and Liberty*, Vol. II: *The Mirage of Social Justice*, p. 64.

6. Robert C. Nichols, "Heredity, Environment, and School Achievement," *Measurement and Evaluation in Guidance*, Vol. 1, No. 2 (Summer 1968), p. 126.

7. Alan Reynolds, *Income and Wealth* (Westport, Connecticut: Greenwood Press, 2006), p. 67.

8. "Choose Your Parents Wisely," *The Economist*, July 26, 2014, pp. 21–22, 25.

9. Friedrich Hayek, *Law, Legislation and Liberty*, Vol. I: *Rules and Order*, Chapter 2.

10. See, for example, Thomas Sowell, *The Quest for Cosmic Justice* (New York: The Free Press, 1999).

11. Friedrich Hayek, *Law, Legislation and Liberty*, Vol. II: *The Mirage of Social Justice*, p. 68.

12. Roscoe Pound, *Criminal Justice in the American City: A Summary* (The Cleveland Foundation, 1922), Part VII, pp. 28–29, 87–88; Roscoe Pound, "The Theory of Judicial Decision. III. A Theory of Judicial Decision for Today," *Harvard Law Review*, Vol. 36,

No. 8 (June 1923), pp. 944, 945, 957; John Dewey, *Human Nature and Conduct: An Introduction to Social Psychology* (New York: Henry Holt and Company, 1922), p. 46.

13. Edmund Burke, *Speeches and Letters on American Affairs* (New York: E.P. Dutton and Company, Inc., 1961), p. 198.

14. Milton and Rose Friedman, *Free to Choose*, p. 148.

15. Friedrich Hayek, *Law, Legislation and Liberty*, Vol. II: *The Mirage of Social Justice*, p. 67.

16. William Godwin, *Enquiry Concerning Political Justice, and Its Influence on Morals and Happiness*, edited by F.E.L. Priestley (Toronto: University of Toronto Press, 1946), Vol. II, p. 419.

17. Bernard Shaw, *The Intelligent Woman's Guide to Socialism and Capitalism* (London: Constable and Company, 1928), p. 254.

18. Ibid., p. 169.

19. Ken Murray, "Genetics, Athletics Mesh for Mannings," *Baltimore Sun*, December 12, 2004, p. 1D.

20. *Public Papers of the Presidents of the United States, Barack Obama: 2013* (Washington: United States Government Publishing Office, 2018), Book II, p. 1331.

21. Herman Kahn, *World Economic Development: 1979 and Beyond* (Boulder, Colorado: Westview Press, 1979), pp. 60–61.

22. "Operation Wealth Speed," *Forbes*, April/May 2021, p. 72.

23. Jonathan I. Israel, *European Jewry in the Age of Mercantilism: 1550–1750* (Oxford: Clarendon Press, 1985), pp. 5–23.

24. Victor Purcell, *The Chinese in Southeast Asia*, second edition (London: Oxford University Pres, 1965), pp. 404n, 472–476, 478, 526–527; Lennox A. Mills, *Southeast Asia: Illusion and Reality in Politics and Economics* (Minneapolis: University of Minnesota Press, 1964), p. 123; J.A.C. Mackie, "Anti-Chinese Outbreaks in Indonesia, 1959–68," *The Chinese in Indonesia*, edited by J.A.C. Mackie (Honolulu: University of Hawaii Press, 1976), pp. 82, 83, 92.

25. "Is Africa Ready for Amin?" *Newsweek*, August 4, 1975, pp. 36, 41; Roger Mann, "Amin Buys Loyalty of Soldiers," *Washington Post*, April 6, 1977, p. A13; Steven Strasser, Helen Gibson, and Ron Moreau, "The Fall of Idi Amin," *Newsweek*, April 23, 1979, pp. 41–42; Pranay B. Gupte, "Picking Up the Pieces in Uganda Is Not Easy," *New York Times*, June 1, 1980, p. E2.

26. Sean Turnell, *Fiery Dragons: Banks, Moneylenders and Microfinance in Burma* (Copenhagen: NIAS Press, 2008), pp. 13–14, 49; Ian Brown, *Burma's Economy in the Twentieth Century* (New York: Cambridge University Press, 2013), pp. 96–97.

27. "Is Africa Ready for Amin?" *Newsweek*, August 4, 1975, pp. 36, 41; Roger Mann, "Amin Buys Loyalty of Soldiers," *Washington Post*, April 6, 1977, p. A13; Steven Strasser, Helen Gibson, and Ron Moreau, "The Fall of Idi Amin," *Newsweek*, April 23, 1979, pp. 41–42; Pranay B. Gupte, "Picking Up the Pieces in Uganda Is Not Easy," *New York Times*, June 1, 1980, p. E2.

28. Sean Turnell, *Fiery Dragons*, p. 193. See also Usha Mahajani, *The Role of Indian Minorities in Burma and Malaya* (Westport, Connecticut: Greenwood Press, 1973), p. 20.

29. Victor Purcell, *The Chinese in Southeast Asia*, second edition, pp. 513, 514n, 515.

30. Solomon Grayzel, *A History of the Jews: From the Babylonian Exile to the End of World War II* (Philadelphia: The Jewish Publication Society of America, 1947), pp. 387–394; Esther Benbassa, *The Jews of France: A History from Antiquity to the Present*, translated by M.B. DeBevoise (Princeton: Princeton University Press, 1999), pp. 15, 16, 20–21; H.H. Ben-Sasson, "The Collapse of Old Settlements and the Establishment of New Ones, 1348–1517," *A History of the Jewish People*, edited by H.H. Ben-Sasson (London: Weidenfeld and Nicolson, 1976), pp. 561–565.

31. Roger P. Bartlett, *Human Capital: The Settlement of Foreigners in Russia, 1762–1804* (New York: Cambridge University Press, 1979), pp. 35, 86–87, 88.

32. Ibid., p. 87.

33. John Stuart Mill, "On Liberty," *Collected Works of John Stuart Mill*, Vol. XVIII: *Essays on Politics and Society*, edited by J.M. Robson (Toronto: University of Toronto Press, 1977), p. 245.

34. See Rob Arnott and Casey B. Mulligan, "How Deadly Were the Covid Lockdowns?" *Wall Street Journal*, January 12, 2023, p. A15; Casey B. Mulligan and Robert D. Arnott, "The Young Were Not Spared: What Death Certificates Reveal about Non-Covid Excess Deaths," *Inquiry*, Vol. 59 (2022), pp. 1–9; Jiaquan Xu, et al., "Mortality in the United States, 2021," *NCHS Data Brief*, No. 456, December 2022, Figure 4, p. 4.

35. Edmund Burke, *Speeches and Letters on American Affairs*, p. 198.

36. U.S. Bureau of the Census, "Poverty Status of Families, by Type of Family, Presence of Related Children, Race, and Hispanic Origin: 1959 to 2020," *Current Population Survey, 1960–2021*, Annual Social and Economic Supplements (CPS ASEC), Table 4.

37. Terry M. Moe, *Special Interest: Teachers Unions and America's Public Schools* (Washington: Brookings Institution Press, 2011), p. 280.

38. Stephan Thernstrom and Abigail Thernstrom, *America in Black and White: One Nation, Indivisible* (New York: Simon & Schuster, 1997), p. 233.

39. Ibid.

40. Hugh Davis Graham, "The Origins of Affirmative Action: Civil Rights and the Regulatory State," *The Annals of the American Academy of Political and Social Science*, Vol. 523 (September 1992), pp. 53, 54.

41. See, for example, Shelby Steele, *The Content of Our Character: A New Vison of Race in America* (New York: St. Martin's Press, 1990); Shelby Steele, *White Guilt: How Blacks and Whites Together Destroyed the Promise of the Civil Rights Era* (New York: HarperCollins, 2006).

42. Shelby Steele, *White Guilt*, p. 123.

43. Ibid., p. 124.

44. Stephan Thernstrom and Abigail Thernstrom, *America in Black and White*, pp. 158–161.

45. James P. Smith and Finis Welch, *Race Differences in Earnings: A Survey and New Evidence* (Santa Monica, California: The Rand Corporation, 1978), pp. 15, 19. See also p. 14.

46. "Civil Rights Act," *New York Times*, July 5, 1964, p. E1.

47. Daniel P. Moynihan, "Employment, Income, and the Ordeal of the Negro Family," *Daedalus*, Vol. 94, No. 4 (Fall 1965), p. 752.

48. Stephan Thernstrom and Abigail Thernstrom, *America in Black and White*, p. 150; *Congressional Record: Senate*, June 19, 1964, p. 14511; E.W. Kenworthy, "Action by Senate: Revised Measure Now Goes Back to House for Concurrence," *New York Times*, June 20, 1964, p. 1; *Congressional Record: House*, July 2, 1964, p. 15897; "House Civil Rights Vote," *New York Times*, July 3, 1964, p. 9; E.W. Kenworthy, "President Signs Civil Rights Bill," *New York Times*, July 3, 1964, pp. 1, 9; *Statistics of the Congressional Election of November 6, 1962* (Washington: United States Government Printing Office, 1963), p. 46; William Anderson, "Predicts G.O.P. Will Capture House in 1964," *Chicago Daily Tribune*, November 20, 1962, p. 8.

49. For documented examples, see Thomas Sowell, *Affirmative Action Around the World: An Empirical Study* (New Haven: Yale University Press, 2004), pp. 11, 13, 26–27, 30–32, 33, 34, 61, 62–63, 69, 120–122.

50. Ibid., p. 32.

51. Ibid., pp. 12–13, 30, 33, 34, 121–122.

52. Ibid., pp. 12, 13, 120, 121.

53. John H. Bunzel, "Affirmative-Action Admissions: How It "Works" at UC Berkeley," *The Public Interest*, Fall 1988, p. 124; National Center for Education Statistics, *The Condition of Education: 1996* (Washington: U.S. Government Printing Office, 1996,) p. 86.

54. John H. Bunzel, "Affirmative-Action Admissions: How It "Works" at UC Berkeley," *The Public Interest*, Fall 1988, p. 125.

55. Richard H. Sander and Stuart Taylor, Jr., *Mismatch: How Affirmative Action Hurts Students It's Intended to Help, and Why Universities Won't Admit It* (New York: Basic Books, 2012), pp. 138, 153, 154.

56. Ibid., p. 154.

57. Ibid.

58. Arthur Hu, "Minorities Need More Support," *The Tech* (M.I.T.), March 17, 1987, pp. 4, 6.

59. Robert Lerner and Althea K. Nagai, *Racial and Ethnic Preferences in Admissions at Five Public Medical Schools* (Washington: Center for Equal Opportunity, 2001), pp. 12, 34–36, 51–52, 71–73, 81–83.

60. Richard H. Sander and Stuart Taylor, Jr., *Mismatch*, p. 231.

61. Ibid., pp. 237–244; Gail Heriot, "A Dubious Expediency," *A Dubious Expediency: How Race Preferences Damage Higher Education*, edited by Gail Heriot and Maimon Schwarzschild (New York: Encounter Books, 2021), pp. 73–74, 75.

62. See, for example, Stephan Thernstrom and Abigail Thernstrom, "Reflections on *The Shape of the River*," *UCLA Law Review*, Vol. 46, No. 5 (June 1999), pp. 1588–1590.

63. Richard H. Sander and Stuart Taylor, Jr., *Mismatch*, pp. 106, 236.

64. Stephan Thernstrom and Abigail Thernstrom, "Reflections on *The Shape of the River*," *UCLA Law Review*, Vol. 46, No. 5 (June 1999), pp. 1583–1631; Richard H. Sander and Stuart Taylor, Jr., *Mismatch*, pp. 106–107, 236–237; Thomas Sowell, *Wealth, Poverty and Politics*, revised and enlarged edition (New York: Basic Books, 2016), pp. 200–203.

65. Merrill Sheils, et al., "Minority Report Card," *Newsweek*, July 12, 1976, pp. 74–75; Bernard D. Davis, "Academic Standards in Medical Schools," *New England Journal of Medicine*, May 13, 1976, pp. 1118–1119; J.W. Foster, "Race and Truth at Harvard," *The New Republic*, July 17, 1976, pp. 16–20. An example of what Professor Davis warned against was Dr. Patrick Chavis, who had been admitted under a minority preference program to the

medical school at the University of California at Davis. Richard H. Sander and Stuart Taylor, Jr., *Mismatch*, p. 195.

66. Thomas Sowell, *A Man of Letters* (New York: Encounter Books, 2007), p. 118.

67. Ibid., p. 107; Thomas Sowell, *A Personal Odyssey* (New York: The Free Press, 2000), pp. 202–203.

68. Gail Heriot, "A Dubious Expediency," *A Dubious Expediency*, edited by Gail Heriot and Maimon Schwarzschild, pp. 46–50, 274–275; Robin Wilson, "Article Critical of Black Students' Qualifications Roils Georgetown U. Law Center," *Chronicle of Higher Education*, April 24, 1991, pp. A33, A35.

69. Richard H. Sander and Stuart Taylor, Jr., *Mismatch*, pp. 158–162.

70. Eric Kelderman, "College Presidents Created a Money Monster. Now Will They Tame It?" *Chronicle of Higher Education*, Volume 68, Issue 12 (February 18, 2022), p. 7; Bill Saporito, "The NCAA Keeps Running Plays Against Pay for Student-Athletes," *Washington Post*, May 25, 2023, p. A19.

71. According to the *Chronicle of Higher Education*, "about half of the athletes in those Division I sports are Black." At colleges where 2.4 percent of the undergraduate student population were black males, they were "55 percent of their football teams and 56 percent of their men's basketball teams." Victoria Jackson, "The NCAA's Farcical Anti-Athlete Argument: The Real 'March Madness' Is the Organization's Work to Deprive Athletes of More Educational Resources," *Chronicle of Higher Education*, Volume 67, Issue 16 (April 16, 2021).

72. Some of the incentives, constraints and patterns in academic institutions are addressed in Thomas Sowell, *Economic Facts and Fallacies*, second edition (New York: Basic Books, 2011), Chapter 4. Brad Wolverton, "NCAA Considers Easing Demands on Athletes' Time," *Chronicle of Higher Education*, Volume 62, Issue 18 (January 15, 2016); Marc Tracy, "N.C.A.A. Declines to Punish North Carolina for Academic Fraud," *New York Times*, October 14, 2017, p. D1. An older account suggests that this sort of thing has been going on for generations. Thomas Sowell, *Inside*

American Education: The Decline, the Deception, the Dogmas (New York: Free Press, 1993), Chapter 9.

73. Richard H. Sander and Stuart Taylor, Jr., *Mismatch*, pp. 220–230.

74. U.S. Department of Health and Human Services, *Health, United States, 2006* (Hyattsville, Maryland: National Center for Health Statistics, 2007), Table 45, p. 228; Barry Latzer, *The Rise and Fall of Violent Crime in America* (New York: Encounter Books, 2016), p. 93.

75. [Daniel Patrick Moynihan], *The Negro Family: The Case for National Action* (Washington: Government Printing Office, 1965), p. 8; Centers for Disease Control and Prevention, U.S. Department of Health and Human Services, "Births: Final Data for 2000," *National Vital Statistics Reports*, Vol. 50, No. 5 (February 12, 2002), Table 19, p. 49.

76. Thomas Sowell, *Affirmative Action Around the World*, pp. 12–13, 30, 33, 34, 61, 62–63, 69.

77. Ibid., pp. 13, 120–122.

78. Reginald G. Damerell, *Education's Smoking Gun: How Teachers Colleges Have Destroyed Education in America* (New York: Freundlich Books, 1985), p. 164.

79. Leonard Buder, "Board Asks Defeat of a Bill Retaining 4 Specialized Schools' Entrance Tests," *New York Times*, May 17, 1971, p. 26.

80. Maria Newman, "Cortines Has Plan to Coach Minorities into Top Schools," *New York Times*, March 18, 1995, p. 1.

81. Fernanda Santos, "Black at Stuy," *New York Times*, February 26, 2012, Metropolitan Desk, p. 6.

82. Donald Harman Akenson, "Diaspora, the Irish and Irish Nationalism," *The Call of the Homeland: Diaspora Nationalisms, Past and Present*, edited by Allon Gal, et al (Leiden: Brill, 2010), pp. 190–191; Michael Ornstein, *Ethno-Racial Inequality in the City of Toronto: An Analysis of the 1996 Census* (Toronto: Access and Equity Unit, City of Toronto, 2000), p. ii.

83. Milton Friedman, "Asian Values: Right..." *National Review,* December 31, 1997, pp. 36–37; Alex Singleton, "Creating a Showplace of Free Markets: Sir John Cowperthwaite," *Fraser Forum,* October 2006, pp. 23–24; William McGurn, "Yes, Minister," *Far Eastern Economic Review,* March 31, 1994, p. 29.

84. "Relax, Mr. Lee," *The Economist,* January 16, 1988, p. 20; "The Wise Man of the East," *The Economist,* March 28, 2015, p. 18; Chun Han Wong and P.R. Venkat, "Singapore's Lee Set Model for Emerging Economies," *Wall Street Journal,* March 23, 2015, p. A1; Daniel Yergin and Joseph Stanislaw, *The Commanding Heights: The Battle for the World Economy* (New York: Touchstone, 2002), pp. 164–168, 183–184.

85. Ethan Epstein, "Democracy, Gangnam-Style," *The Weekly Standard,* December 17, 2012, pp. 23–26; David Ekbladh, "How to Build a Nation," *The Wilson Quarterly,* Vol. 28, No. 1 (Winter 2004), pp. 19–20; Norman Pearsltine, "How South Korea Surprised the World," *Forbes,* April 30, 1979, pp. 53 ff.

86. Gurcharan Das, "India Unbound," *The American Spectator,* Summer Reading Issue 2001, pp. 36–38; Rakesh Mohan, "India at the Crossroads," *Far Eastern Economic Review,* March 2, 2000, p. 34.

87. "Capitalism with Chinese Characteristics," *The Economist,* November 28, 1992, special survey on China, pp. 6–8; "Enter the Dragon," *The Economist,* March 10, 2001, pp. 23–25; "The Fruits of Growth," *The Economist,* January 2, 2021, pp. 28–29.

88. Oliver Wendell Holmes, *Collected Legal Papers* (New York: Peter Smith, 1952), p. 293.

89. Paul Johnson, *The Quotable Paul Johnson: A Topical Compilation of His Wit, Wisdom and Satire,* edited by George J. Marlin, et al (New York: Farrar, Strauss and Giroux, 1994), p. 138.

INDEX